T0394112

"In his usual clearly written and well-structured way, Dr. Grieger has written a gem of a book. The title is the clue: if you want to be happy, you need to take the project seriously and put in the work. If you bring these qualities to the book and follow Dr. Grieger's guidelines, then you will be healthier and happier than you would be if you just passively read the book. The choice is yours!"

– Windy Dryden, PhD, emeritus professor,
Psychotherapeutic Studies, Goldsmiths University of London.

"In *The Serious Business of Being Happy,* Russell Grieger systematically addresses the most important question any human being could conceivably ask: how to become and stay happy. Not a one-size-fits-all approach, Dr. Grieger helps readers uniquely fashion their 'passionate purpose' in life, and then compassionately guides them in building rational-emotive-behavioral strategies for overcoming obstacles to this self-chosen end; identifying ethical principles to direct this purpose; and creating and implementing a 'happiness action plan'. Chock full of workshops, Grieger shows the reader how to plot a clearheaded path to personal and professional fulfilment. Highly recommended for psychotherapists and laypersons alike."

– Elliot D. Cohen, PhD, founder of Logic-Based Therapy;
author of Making Peace with Imperfection.

"This book is a beauty. Not a pollyannaistic account of what it takes to be happy, it flags what we can do to get on the road to happiness by '*acting in accordance with your passionate purpose, grounded in rational thought about yourself, other people, and life in general, and guided by your sacred principles.*' It is a banquet full of Russell Grieger's amazing insights into the mindset needed for happiness-producing action."

"In this practical book, Dr. Russell Grieger shows that wisdom and happiness are within the grasp of anyone who responsibly acts to pursue purposeful, meaningful, and attainable goals. In this process he ably shows how to narrow down happiness goals and follow through. He identifies happiness-sabotaging negative beliefs and how to combat them. By using Dr. Grieger's carefully mapped action plans, you'll increase your range of positive experiences, build resilience against adversity, advance your enlightened personal and social interests, and add joy to your life and to the lives of those close to you."

THE SERIOUS BUSINESS
OF BEING HAPPY

The Serious Business of Being Happy combines scientific research and clinical experience to lay out a wealth of strategies to bring about happiness with oneself, other people, and daily life in general.

Suitable for a wide range of mental health professionals, the book provides an applicable, comprehensive step-by-step approach to fulfilling a happy life. Chapters draw on Rational Emotive Behavior Therapy and Cognitive Behavior Therapy theory and practice to illustrate key areas where happiness can be maximized, including identifying life purpose and sacred principles, finding happiness with oneself, and finding happiness with others. Also included is a personalized "Happiness Action Plan," along with case examples, exercises, and reflections, to translate the ideas into concrete action.

Leaving aside the psychobabble and feel-good clichés, *The Serious Business of Being Happy* is a valuable resource for practitioners working with individuals to build a positive psychology in everyday life.

Russell Grieger, PhD, is a licensed clinical psychologist with more than thirty-five years of experience treating individuals, couples, and families with Rational Emotive Behavior Therapy.

THE SERIOUS BUSINESS OF BEING HAPPY

A Cognitive Behavior Workbook to Bring
Happiness to Every Day of Life

Russell Grieger

Routledge
Taylor & Francis Group

NEW YORK AND LONDON

First published 2020
by Routledge
52 Vanderbilt Avenue, New York, NY 10017

and by Routledge
2 Park Square, Milton Park, Abingdon, Oxon, OX14 4RN

Routledge is an imprint of the Taylor & Francis Group, an informa business

© 2020 Taylor & Francis

Library of Congress Cataloging-in-Publication Data
A catalog record for this title has been requested

ISBN: 978-1-138-38633-4 (hbk)
ISBN: 978-1-138-38634-1 (pbk)
ISBN: 978-0-429-42685-8 (ebk)

Typeset in Baskerville
by Deanta Global Publishing Services, Chennai, India

Printed and bound by CPI Group (UK) Ltd, Croydon, CR0 4YY

For
My sons, Todd and Gabriel,
whose love and loyalty
warm each and every one of my days.

CONTENTS

ACKNOWLEDGMENTS

What is found in this book represents a fount of knowledge accumulated over a lifetime from far too many people to acknowledge.

Nevertheless, I do want to highlight two giants whose contributions have been enormous, Albert Ellis and Stephen Covey. Their thinking has so saturated mine that sometimes I don't know where theirs ends and mine begins. I heartily recognize them, applaud them, thank them.

I also want to acknowledge the two Jays in my life. Jay Varner helped enormously with the early drafts of this book, especially with regard to Part I, where he refined both my ideas and grammar. Jay Kauffmann put his mark on the later stages, editing each and every page. They each polished awkward sentences, garbled paragraphs, and murky ideas, not to mention raising cogent content questions. transforming them into ones that are coherent and readable. Thank you, guys. You made me sound better than I ever could on my own.

I especially want to express my gratitude to my wife, Patti. She not only typed and retyped every single page, but she blessed me with a steady stream of support, encouragement, and affection every step of the way. I extend to her a million "thank yous," along with an ocean of love.

AUTHOR NOTES

- All names and identifying data/characteristics, except those of my own family, have been changed, all to protect the privacy and anonymity of the people in this book.
- Much of the content of this book, particularly "Part II: The Happiness Practices," reflect ideas originally published in my Psychology Today blog, *Happiness on Purpose*.

ABOUT THE AUTHOR

Russell Grieger, PhD, is a licensed clinical psychologist with a robust private practice in Charlottesville, Virginia. He provides psychotherapy to individuals, couples, and families, and he facilitates well-being growth groups.

In addition, Russ has over thirty-five years' experience helping individuals and organizations fulfill their mission and reach their potential for sustainable high performance. Having consulted and provided programs on such diverse topics as Developing Organizational Vision and Direction, Team Building, Motivation, Conflict Resolution, Managing Change, Effective Organizational Communication, and Stress Management, he has been a pioneer in helping organizations create and sustain a culture of personal responsibility and accountability and in leadership growth and development.

Russ received his undergraduate degree from the University of Evansville, where he played on two consecutive NCAA Championship basketball teams, and his Master's and Doctoral degrees from The Ohio State University. An Adjunct Professor at the University of Virginia, he has authored eight professional books; over fifty chapters and articles; a series of self-help audiocassettes; two recent books for the layperson, including *The Couples Therapy Companion* and *Developing Unrelenting Drive, Dedication, and Determination*; and a memoir, *The Perfect Season*. He lives with his wife and son in both Charlottesville, Virginia, and St. Thomas in the U.S. Virgin Islands.

INTRODUCTION

Welcome to *The Serious Business of Being Happy: A Cognitive Behavior Workbook to Bring Happiness to Every Day of Life*. I very much look forward to guiding you in this journey.

Before we begin, I want you to know that I hold the topic of happiness near and dear to my heart. All told, I've now devoted over thirty-five years as a practitioner of Rational Emotive Behavior Therapy (REBT) to helping people both rid themselves of personal misery and build a life filled with happiness. I think of the accomplished engineer caught in the grip of depression and alcohol, the nurse stricken by such severe bouts of anxiety she feared she might lose her job, the social worker who could neither shake her anger against the man who molested her nor the guilt she carried for not reporting him to the police. Then there was the college professor who, awash in the world of Internet pornography, left his wife for a favorite escort, the housewife tormented by an abusive husband who she was too fearful to leave, and the promiscuous college student with such low self-esteem that she used her body to garner the attention and affection she needed to feel good about herself.

The list goes on and on. Just like you, and everyone else for that matter, these lost souls longed for happiness. They had the desire, but what they didn't have was an understanding of what brought on their misery. Neither did they have a clue as to how to bring about the personal happiness they so craved.

But I did. And I devoted every ounce of my energy to helping them learn the exact REBT concepts and strategies they needed to help them bring themselves both peace-of-mind and emotional well-being.

And, that's why I wrote this book: To guide all of you who wish to fill your daily life with happiness, whether you want to work independently on your own or in tandem with your psychotherapist, counselor, or life coach. I also wrote this book for my colleagues – the psychologists, counselors, social workers, psychiatrists, psychiatric nurses, life coaches, and family physicians – who want to add REBT strategies to their therapeutic toolbox.

So, to all of you, welcome. I know the principles and practices I will share with you work. I have successfully used them with every one of my patients through my years of clinical practice, as well as with myself in my own personal life. Whether you are a layperson or a helping professional, all you have to do is bring your integrity, energy, and commitment to this endeavor. Now, with that said, let me orient you to this labor of love.

REBT and Happiness

The wise of us guide our practices by sound principles. Take, for example, the U.S. federal government. At their best, members of Congress craft the laws of the land consistent with the articles of the U.S. Constitution. Similarly, leaders of great as opposed to merely good companies adhere to their "sacred principles" as they go about making their critical business decisions (Collins, 2001). In this same vein, we mental health professionals strive to provide our services within the ethical canons laid down by our respective disciplines.

Similarly, the five Rational Emotive Behavior Therapy principles that follow serve as a guide for both you practitioners and you laypeople in the quest for happiness. They will help you choose from the best possible strategies to help create a happy life.

The Purpose of Life

Rational Emotive Behavior Therapy is agnostic with regard to the purpose of life. It agrees with such existential philosophers as Martin Heidegger (2018), Albert Camus (1942), and John Paul Sartre (1943), who argue that there may very well be no overarching purpose to life. We are born, live a certain period of time, and then no longer exist. This appeals to we REBTers because, with no general or particular meaning to life, people can freely create their own personal meaning and then passionately live it.

Nevertheless, REBT readily acknowledges that if indeed there is a purpose to life, then surely it must be to be happy. Its reasoning starts with the logic of Aristotle. He observed that all human desires ultimately serve the purpose of finding happiness. For example, if my goal is to create and maintain a vibrant clinical practice, I will work toward that goal in order to make a good living, derive daily satisfaction, and be of service to other human beings. But if I ask, "Why do I want to achieve all that?," then the honest answer is ultimately to be happy.

Consider your own life and see if you don't find the same to be true for you as well. No matter what you may want out of your life – loving relationships, financial security, a cozy dwelling – don't you covet it in order to be happy? Harkening back to Aristotle, happiness turns out to be the only goal that is an end unto itself. No one wants to be happy in order to achieve their other ends.

But that's not all. Dr Albert Ellis (Ellis & Becker, 1982), the founder of Rational Emotive Behavior Therapy, provides empirical evidence to support the logic of Aristotle. He noted that all people across the globe share two major life goals: (1) to survive; (2) to be happy while surviving. If this is true, then the goal of REBT, and all other forms of Cognitive Behavioral Therapy, is likewise twofold: One is to free people from the ravages of their dysfunctional emotions and behaviors; the second is to help them weave happiness into the fabric of their lives in the form of pleasure, satisfaction, contentment, peace of mind, and emotional well-being.

The bottom line is for you laypeople to embrace happiness as the purpose of your life. And I urge you mental health professionals to fervently encourage your charges to unabashedly adopt this purpose for themselves.

Happiness Defined

Once one decides to make happiness the primary goal of life, then it becomes important to understand exactly what happiness is. With this understanding, one will be well positioned to select the best methods to create such a joy-filled life.

After reflecting upon this for a good part of my professional life, I have come to embrace the following definition of happiness:

> Happiness is acting in accordance with your passionate purpose, grounded in rational thought about yourself, other people, and life in general, and guided by your sacred principles.

An intriguing definition, no? But also useful. Let me break it down so it can be put into practice.

Happiness

In contrast to pleasure, which has to do with a positive experience in a given moment, happiness relates to the quality of one's life as a whole. When one says, "I'm happy," one does not mean he or she just has occasional good times, nor does it mean that one feels happy all the time, for that is utopian or perfectionistic. No, this person means that life is rewarding and satisfying as a whole, that one has a life in which one prospers and flourishes despite occasional setbacks or frustrations, that one lives a life he or she loves to live. This is exactly what we're after in this book.

Acting

Acting means doing. Think about it. You can't mow your lawn by sitting in a chair and wishing or hoping it will get mowed; you have to get up, go outside, and mow it. Similarly, there is no way you can work yourself into good physical condition by sitting on the couch and watching TV. No, you have to get off your duff and work out. It's the same with happiness. To be happy, you must do what is necessary to bring happiness into your life. You must act, act, act. That's where passionate purpose, rational thinking, and ethics come into play, for they give order and direction to your actions.

Passionate Purpose

It may be a cliché, but it's true that all people long to lead a meaningful life – to be part of something bigger than themselves, to feel their life has significance, that they matter. To grace life with happiness, then, one needs to orient his or her life beyond just paying the bills, putting in a solid day's work, keeping the house clean. When one connects what one does in life – each and every day – to something bigger than just oneself, this person will feel fulfilled most every day and go to sleep each night feeling satisfied and content.

Rational Thought

As you will soon see, we all possess a fallible mind, one that all too easily thinks illogically and irrationally, thereby bringing on the variety of negative emotions that destroys happiness. The bottom line is that, to find happiness, one must cultivate thought habits, beliefs, and paradigms that prompt happiness – with and about oneself, other people, and life in general.

Ethical Principles

To be happy means to not only act to fulfill a passionate purpose, but to do so based on principles that put us in good stead with ourselves, those with whom we interact, and our community at large. In the short run, acting unethically may provide us short-range gratification, but it almost always leads to unhappiness in the long run.

So, this definition of happiness, in my opinion, captures all the ingredients needed for a person to live a happy, fulfilled life. If one will only take the time to carve out and act according to a passionate purpose, habitually think rationally about oneself, other people, and life in general, and adhere to their ethical principles, one will most likely be filled with energy and enthusiasm, will maximize productivity across the spectrum of life, and regularly feel satisfied and fulfilled most of the time.

Enlightened Self-Interest

As you will see in Part I of this book, creating a happy life can be very challenging. To sustain the effort needed to power past these challenges and create happiness, one would be wise to live by the principle of *Enlightened Self-Interest.*

To fully appreciate what *Enlightened Self-Interest* means, let me contrast it with two other principles that commonly drive people to seek psychological help. The first is *Selfishness,* a principle that is core to both the narcissist and the anti-social personality. Captured in sentence form, this principle would sound like this: "When there is a conflict between what I want and what you want, only I matter, not you, so I'll meet my needs regardless of the consequences for you." A person holding this perspective then characteristically acts in an uncaring, self-centered, and even ruthless manner to satisfy one's own desires. The hell with others. The result may be immediate gratification, but it often incurs the enduring animosity of loved ones, friends, and colleagues that will curtail the possibility for sustained happiness.

The mirror opposite of selfishness is *Selflessness.* Common to people of low self-esteem, those desperate for approval, and/or those fearing dissension, this principal states: "When there is a conflict between what I want and what you want, I don't matter as much as you, so I'll sacrifice my desires for yours." In addition to suffering the emotional deflation attendant to holding such a self-denigrating belief, acting selflessly diminishes one's pleasure, invites self-flagellation, and sets one up for being taken advantage of by others. Obviously, this person's happiness suffers.

The principle of *Enlightened Self-Interest* positions one with the best chance to create a happy life. This principle starts with the conviction that no one is placed on this earth to look after my happiness. It's totally my responsibility, no one else's. Therefore, it goes on, while I am no more important than anyone else, I will hold myself to be more important to me than I will hold others, but I will be careful to put others a very close second so that I always consider their well-being as well as my own. By operating on this principle, one will always look out for oneself, while neither sacrificing for nor running roughshod over others.

The ABCs of Happiness

I will discuss the ABCs of happiness at great length in Chapter 3. In brief, we Rational Emotive Behavior Therapy practitioners assert that the main cause of both happiness and unhappiness does not directly result from one's circumstances, but from the beliefs one holds about them. According to REBT, then, the mood one experiences (labeled the C), whether happy or unhappy, transient or enduring, can to some degree be influenced by one's life circumstances (the A), but, most significantly, by the enduring beliefs one holds and endorses about them (labeled the B). Consider the recent suicides of designer Kate Spade and TV personality Anthony Bourdain. They had all the worldly trappings of happiness they could ever want, so the despair they felt had to come from their negative, despairing mindsets.

In REBT, we first help people track down and destroy those beliefs that bring about their unhappiness. Then we lead them to adopt ones that will cause them to experience feelings of satisfaction, well-being, and happiness. Almost all unhappy people hold negative, irrational, and dysfunctional beliefs about themselves, others, and/or their life circumstances, while happy people hold affirming and realistic beliefs with regard to themselves, their fellow travelers, and their life circumstances.

So, as I tell my patients with tongue in cheek, the bottom line is that there is both bad and good news. The bad news is that they've largely brought on their own unhappiness by virtue of their own negative, irrational thinking. But the good news is the same – they've brought on their own unhappiness by virtue of their own negative, irrational thinking. This is good news because, while people may not be able to change the negative circumstances in their lives, they can always change the way they think and thereby bring themselves both relief from misery and an infusion of happiness. The bottom line is that there is always hope for creating happiness, no matter the adverse circumstances, if only they'll take the responsibility to do it.

Hard Work

One of the myths that persists in some psychotherapy circles is that insight is curative. Holding this myth, these psychotherapists use such techniques as free association, dream analysis, and the relationship between the therapist and the patient to sneak past a person's defenses in order to bring repressed memories, associations, and feelings to the light of day. Once the patient clearly sees all this, the myth says, symptoms then dissipate and cure is affected.

We now know that this is simply not true. As the acclaimed psychologist Carl Rogers (1951) famously said, "Insight is necessary but not sufficient." Indeed, the beliefs a person holds that both cause misery and block happiness are readily accessible, most often within the first treatment session. Once these are uncovered, then the real work of psychotherapy begins. Now the job is to help the patient appreciate the relevance of these beliefs in causing the unhappiness and guide him or her to renounce and replace them. It is when a person relinquishes the misery-creating beliefs and adopts new happiness-driving ones that elegant change takes place.

I make it a practice to emphasize to my patients that, to rid unhappiness and find happiness, they must put in daily work, not just attend the forty-five-minute weekly session we spend together. They cannot afford to be a spectator in their lives, sitting back in the bleachers and watching events unfold before them. They must work long and hard at it.

I cannot overstate the importance of this. I believe that I do have a certain amount of knowledge and skill, but I am the first to admit that I have no magic. It is when my patients diligently apply themselves to the change process – that is, when they work, work, work – that positive results happen. Without this sustained effort, change will either come glacially slow or not at all.

So, you clinicians have it on your shoulders to repeatedly emphasize the necessity of hard work to your charges. And you laypeople have no choice but to work long and hard to first dislodge those beliefs and actions that bring on your unhappiness and then engrain new ones to bring on the happiness you understandably crave.

The Happiness Process

Armed with the foregoing Rational Emotive Behavior Therapy principles, *The Serious Business of Being Happy* provides a step-by-step guide to bring happiness to each day of life. Replete with powerful, proven strategies to translate concepts into concrete action, it is divided into four major parts.

Part I: The Happiness Foundation

Part I puts the reader right to work. Both informational and action-oriented, it lays the necessary foundation for the crafting of a personalized Happiness Action Plan (HAP) that is started in Part II, *The Happiness Practices*, and is finalized in Part III of *The Serious Business of Being Happy*. It emphasizes the need to assume total responsibility to bring happiness to one's life – consciously, conscientiously, and deliberately.

Chapter 1: The Happiness Challenges

An accurate description of one's current happiness challenges is the starting point. This chapter guides the reader to clearly define the happiness challenges now faced that need to be overcome to create the happy, fulfilled life wanted.

Chapter 2: Visioning Happiness

Stephen Covey, the author of *The 7 Habits of Highly Effective People* (1989), wisely tells us to always begin with the end in mind. Following his advice, this chapter guides the reader to create a clear vision of what a happy life will look like, as one wants it. By seeing this, the person can informatively select the best strategies to get there, feel energized and hopeful about success, and know when and where to make mid-course corrections.

Chapter 3: The Happiness Mindsets

With a clear picture of the gap between where one is and where one wants to be, Chapter 3 discusses five core mindsets necessary for a person to generate and sustain the effort needed to make the happiness vision a reality. Adopting these mindsets will empower one to persistently act on the strategies selected in Part II to create life happiness.

Part II: The Happiness Practices

The five chapters that comprise Part II provide both the clinician and the layperson the cognitive and behavioral strategies to create a happy, fulfilled life. Each chapter first guides the reader in how to master a Breakthrough Strategy that then opens the door to the effective use of the additional cognitive and behavioral strategies to follow. The reader can select from these strategies to build a comprehensive, personalized Happiness Action Plan (HAP) to be finalized in Part III.

Chapter 4: Live Your Passionate Purpose

When people possess a passionate purpose for their life, they wake up each morning invigorated, go through their day energized, and put their head on the pillow at night with a sense of satisfaction. This chapter leads the reader through a three-step process to create his or her own passionate purpose and a process to manifest it throughout daily life. By doing so, this person can perceive life to be meaningful, significant, and important, which are all core ingredients to being happy.

Chapter 5: Happiness with Yourself

Chapter 5 first introduces the reader to the Breakthrough Strategy of Unconditional Self-Acceptance, a lack of which has caused a huge percentage of all human misery. Then, through both clinical examples and cogent exercises, this chapter teaches the reader how to adopt such a perspective for oneself. It concludes by providing ten additional powerful practices – five cognitive and five behavioral – that can further the experience of happiness with oneself on a daily basis.

Chapter 6: Happiness with Others

We don't live on a desert island. We live with and among other human beings, some of whom provide us immense pleasure, while others frustrate and disappoint us. This chapter teaches REBT's Breakthrough Strategy of Premeditated Acceptance and Forgiveness, a paradigm that eliminates the happiness-contaminating emotions of hurt, anger, and bitterness toward others. Without these happiness-contaminating emotions, one can then use some or all of the ten additional strategies – again, five cognitive and five behavioral – to create happiness with those with whom we travel on life's journey.

Chapter 7: Happiness with Life

Life inevitably places unwanted hassles, hardships, and even tragedies in our lap. While we would be wise to rid ourselves of those we can, we had better also learn the REBT Breakthrough Strategy of High Hardship Tolerance (HHT). HHT gives the reader the perspective to gracefully tolerate these inevitable frustrations and discomforts. This chapter then provides five cognitive and five behavioral strategies to keep unhappiness at bay, while also instilling one's life with pleasure and happiness, despite its inevitable adversities. The chapter concludes with the reader selecting strategies to add to one's burgeoning Happiness Action Plan.

Chapter 8: Live Your Ethical Principles

Ethics are a set of moral principles that guide an individual's behavior across situations. Knowing these principles – and acting upon them – aids and abets decision-making, garners the trust of others, and fosters self-confidence. Chapter 8 leads the reader to define one's ethical principles, identifying those situations where it is paramount to act on them, and supporting the reader with additional strategies to keep those principles alive.

Part III: Your Happiness Action Plan

The daily effort the patient makes between psychotherapy sessions is as valuable to therapeutic gain as the effort made during sessions. Such daily work is also crucial for the creation of a happy life. Therefore, those who have a clear idea of what they need to think and do to be happy have the best chance of experiencing happiness a healthy portion of their time.

Chapter 9: Creating Your Happiness Action Plan

Drawing on the strategies presented in Chapters 4 through 8, this chapter guides the reader to finalize their Happiness Action Plan, detailing exactly what they will do to bring happiness to their lives and precisely planning when, where, and with whom they will do it. Both the clinician and the layperson now possess the blueprint to build a life filled with happiness. The only thing lacking is follow-through.

Part IV: Sustaining Happiness for Life

Experienced REBT clinicians understand that only through sustained action can a person maintain desired results. Accordingly, to sustain a happy life, a person must continue to act to bring about their happiness. Part IV coaches the reader in how to use both psychological and philosophical tools needed to sustain the effort to continue to lead to a happiness-filled life.

Chapter 10: Sustaining Happiness Action: The Psychological Way

Chapter 10 delves deeply into the psychology of motivation. It teaches powerful, proven strategies to spur one to act to produce valued results. These include the use of rewards and punishments, enrolling supportive others, and both savoring and celebrating happiness.

Chapter 11: Sustaining Happiness Action: The Philosophic Way

Shakespeare said: "It is not in the stars to hold our destiny, but in ourselves." Indeed, those who succeed in living a life filled with happiness embody the philosophical paradigm of Unconditional Personal Responsibility (UPR). This paradigm drives one to act in order to produce intended results, despite difficult circumstances. This chapter grounds the reader in UPR so he or she is well-positioned to lead over time a happy life, no matter the adversity.

Epilogue

The Epilogue summarizes the book, inspires the reader to sustain the strategies that form their Happiness Action Plan, and supplies additional resources to pursue life's happiness. An invitation is tendered to contact the author by email to answer any questions.

Going Forward

I invite you to think of this book as a banquet. I've brought the feast – the perspectives, principles, and practices to help you bring happiness to every day of your life. However, you, the reader, will need to pick up and use the utensils. If you use them, they will allow you, both you clinical colleagues and you laypeople, to devour every morsel you can from *The Serious Business of Being Happy*.

Be Adventuresome and Fun-Loving

I assume that you picked up this book to help bring happiness into your own or someone else's life. A word of caution, however: It is important to not approach this endeavor in a state of desperation or urgency, for these emotional states can hamper your progress. So, take a deep breath. Relax. Look upon the process of building a happy life as an adventure. Pursue this book as an opportunity to experiment with different strategies that can help make pleasure, piece of mind, and satisfaction a way of life. Above all, be fun-loving.

Be Open

Many years ago, I attended a weeklong seminar that turned out to be a monumental dud, except for one invaluable discovery tidbit – I learned the distinction between ignorance and blindness. The seminar leader defined blindness as a state of mind in which we don't know, but we also don't know that we don't know. He went on to say that this is quite a barrier for growth and change, in that, when we don't know and don't know we don't know, we automatically assume that we know. This "already knowing" state blocks our openness to new and potentially valuable ideas.

He then went on to define ignorance as a mindset by which we don't know, but know that we don't know. Knowing that we don't know is a powerful perspective to take, he emphasized, because it opens us up to the possibility for new insights, personal growth, even transformation.

I'm sure, dear reader, that you are bright, accomplished, and knowledgeable. However, I urge you to suspend the "I already know" attitude and assume the "I don't know" one. You can then entertain the possibility that the new information I share may be of value to you.

Be Committed and Responsible

The truth is, you and only you are responsible for the choices you make. In other words, you always have a choice, and you are the chooser of every choice you choose. You are therefore totally responsible for the results you produce or don't produce in your life.

This is a daunting, yet wonderfully empowering fact. If you take seriously your responsibility to act on the insights and strategies this book has to offer, you can attain the happiness I know you desire. So, choose to energetically engage the material in this book, reflect on how you can use it to your advantage, and, above all, act to integrate the strategies into the fabric of your life. Can you experience more happiness? I know you can. Will you? That's up to you.

Onward

The feast now awaits. To you clinicians, my aim is to arm you with the requisite Rational Emotive Behavior Therapy principles and practices to help those entrusted in your hands to find their happiness. And, to you laypeople, I support you in your noble and worthy quest to bring happiness to your life. It will take work and effort, but I know that you can do it. Utilize your tools, keep at it, and you'll see the results.

To each of you, I am honored to serve you with this book. Thank you for putting your trust in me. Please feel free to contact me at any time if I can be of service.

Bon appétit.

PART I

THE HAPPINESS FOUNDATION

Most people who first walk into my office suffer from a severe depression and/or a debilitating anxiety, perhaps a crippling dissociative disorder or even PTSD, or possibly some soul-killing addiction. In meeting these people, I know that my first step is to precisely define the problem: What exactly are the symptoms the person experiences? About who or what is the person unhappy? What are the thoughts, beliefs, or paradigms that may cause his or her misery? In clinical circles, we call this process a psychodiagnosis.

For the purpose of this book, however, I want you to think of your first step toward happiness not as a psychodiagnosis but as a strategic planning process. Let me illustrate what this is with a brief case study from my organizational consulting practice. Some years ago, the physicians from a large medical group requested that I help them become more competitive in their local marketplace. To do that, they and I sequestered ourselves at a mountain ski lodge for an entire weekend – Friday evening and all day Saturday and Sunday. The task I set for them over the course of this weekend was fivefold (see Figure 0.1): First, to precisely define their current undesirable reality; second, to craft a vision of what their practice would look like in the future if it was perfect, exactly as they wanted; third, to adopt the necessary mindsets for success; fourth, to devise a strategic action plan to close the gap between where their practice currently was to where they wanted it to be; and fifth, to systematically and relentlessly implement the plan over the next year.

To my gratification, all twenty-five physicians worked diligently. When Sunday evening rolled around, they had crafted a well-thought-out action plan to reach the results they wanted. Within the allotted twelve months, they had succeeded beyond their wildest dreams. In addition to providing even better patient care than before, they now offered a host of new services, including in-house blood testing, EKGs, and prenatal care, as well as several others. As a result, they not only became the gold standard of family medicine in their community, but they also increased their revenue many-fold in the process.

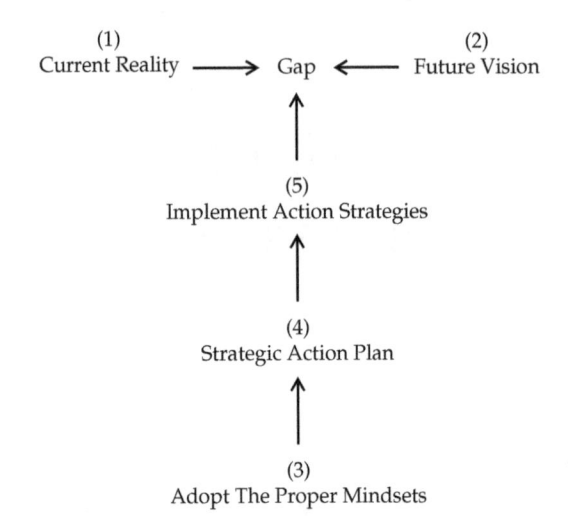

Figure 0.1 The Strategic Planning Process

I share this story to illustrate the process of strategic happiness planning you will follow in this book. In Part I of *The Serious Business of Being Happy,* The Happiness Foundation, I will guide you through the first three strategic planning steps. Chapter 1 helps you define your current happiness reality – the good, the bad, the ugly. Then, in Chapter 2, I lead you through the process of creating a vision of what your happy life would look like if it were perfect, as you wanted it to be. To conclude Part I, I will then share with you the five mindsets you will need to adopt to do the work to turn your happiness vision into a reality. After that, in Parts II and III of this book, to follow, I guide you to develop your own strategic Happiness Action Plan, followed by powerful strategies in Part IV to help you sustain the action to make it happen. One more thing. At the end of each chapter is a page on which you can make notes so as not to forget ideas you find especially helpful to building the happy life you want.

There it is. Let's launch.

1

THE HAPPINESS CHALLENGES

The eighteenth-century philosopher Voltaire certainly got it right when he famously said, "This is not the best of all possible worlds." Indeed, hardships abound. Something can unexpectedly block your path at the most inopportune time. Hassles may arise from the most unexpected source. You might get knocked off balance out of the blue.

Indeed, there are at least three formidable categories of roadblocks that can challenge your happiness anytime, at any place. They are: (1) We live in a difficult world; (2) we do not live among saints or angels; (3) we operate with a fallible human mind. Using these categories, I now provide you an opportunity in the following workshop to lay the first cornerstone of building your strategic Happiness Action Plan – getting a clear picture of your current happiness reality. In doing it, I urge you to follow three simple guidelines.

1. Be courageous. Some of what you will be asked to reflect upon may be unpleasant or unsettling. Don't be afraid to face whatever that may be, for this information can be used to create and act on the Happiness Action Plan you will create further on in this book.
2. Be hopeful. There is absolutely no reason why you can't bring much more happiness into your life – if, that is, you're willing to put in the thought, time, and energy to make it so. Be confident that this is true for you, as it has been for countless others before you. Throw yourself into this first step in your path to happiness with hope.
3. Be committed. As I previously said, and will say again, getting from where you are to where you want to be will take effort and action on your part. The more drive, dedication, and determination you bring to this workshop will give you the best chance for success down the road. Throw yourself into these prompts with commitment.

Now forge ahead to the workshop.

The Happiness Challenges Workshop

Challenge One: We Live in a Difficult World. Life is full of hassles and hardships that, unfortunately, don't always strike at the most convenient moments. A few years back, while vacationing in the Caribbean, a pang of discomfort struck my lower back. *Great! Kidney stones!* I thought. The pain persisted, so, once I returned home to Virginia, I headed straight to my urologist's office. A kidney stone, all right – in fact, three big, nasty ones lined up in a tight row like railroad cars that blocked drainage from my one existing kidney. With kidney failure looming, I needed emergency surgery. Immediately. The doctor rushed me into the operating room only to discover that scar tissue blocked the surgeon's path to reach the stones. In the end, the whole process required a five-day hospital stay, plus three more surgeries – one to drain the backed-up fluid out of my kidney, another to remove the scar tissue, and a final one to remove the stones. Life didn't return to normal until three weeks later.

Naturally, this kidney stone drama took center stage in my life. And, if that wasn't enough, during those three weeks of recovery, I learned that my brother needed heart valve surgery, a good buddy from college discovered he had bladder cancer, and another close friend's marriage fell apart. Needless to say, during this time I thought, *Happiness? What happiness?*

I cannot help but believe that everyone has stories similar to mine. No matter who we are, life offers each of us a steady stream of annoyances, frustrations, and yes, sometimes even tragedies. Not for some of us, but for all of us. These may be our health or our finances, perhaps a marital conflict, some career or employment problem, the need to care for an aging parent, or a son or daughter deployed in a war zone somewhere in the Middle East. This is all of our lot, sooner or later.

Prompt One: Identifying Happiness Blocking Adversities. With that said, list below three troublesome adversities that currently exist in your life. For each, articulate the negative impact it has on your happiness. Then, in the spirit of "If it's going to be, it's up to me," consider what you might do to alter the situation to make it more palatable, rid it from your life, or change your attitude so as to not let it get under your skin.

	Adversity	Negative Impact	Action Strategy
1.	_____	_____	_____
	_____	_____	_____
2.	_____	_____	_____
	_____	_____	_____
3.	_____	_____	_____
	_____	_____	_____

Challenge Two: We Do Not Live Among Saints or Angels. How true. We live among imperfect, fallible human beings who frequently act foolishly and, on occasion, treat us badly. Whether they are within our inner circle or are more distant from us, they will fairly often commit sins of commission, doing things we don't like, and sins of omission, not doing things we do like.

A few months ago, I drove the sixty miles south from Charlottesville to Lynchburg, Virginia, to meet a dear friend for lunch. It was a beautiful Saturday drive with gold and red fall foliage lining the whole route. I arrived five minutes before noon to meet him at the designated restaurant. 12:10. 12:20, then 12:30. No Mike. A phone call produced a recorded message. It turned out that he completely forgot our luncheon. I wasted three hours of precious weekend time driving back and forth for nothing.

How many times has your husband or wife forgot to complete that task they promised to do? Have you ever had the experience of loaning money to a friend or relative who dawdled in paying you back? Or how about that teenager you so lovingly raised who now dismissively says, "Whatever," to your slightest suggestion.

And these are the people who love and care about you. Then there are those people you only know casually or don't know it all. I think about my patient, Chloe, the manager of a large apartment complex who finds herself the recipient of daily venomous complaints from the residents. Then there's Jerry, an X-ray technician who was called racist by two members of his book club because of his political persuasion. Or Glen, an associate professor of sociology, who frequently suffers the indignities of prejudice because of his African American heritage.

The bottom line is that we do not live among saints or angels. But there's more to it than simply that. Not only will these fallible people misbehave, they will do so when, where, and how they do, not just when we find it convenient or permissible. At any moment, given their innate fallibility, the people in our lives may behave thoughtlessly, rudely, insensitively, selfishly, and, yes, even cruelly – regardless of time, place, or circumstance.

All of that is the bad news. But here's the good: We need not be the helpless victim of all that. We can eliminate some of the difficult people who populate our lives. We can attempt to change the obnoxious behavior of some of them. And, of course, when these two options don't work, we can always work to change our attitude, so that the actions of others don't get too deeply under our skin.

Prompt Two: Identifying Difficult People. This takes us to your next prompt. Identify the people who challenge your happiness. List the top three. For each, note what emotional and/or behavioral ways you react to them that undercuts your happiness? What might you do to rid this person from your life, change his or her behavior so as not to be so difficult for you, and/or change the way you think so you can let his or her behavior slide off your back.

	Difficult Person	Your Reaction	Action Strategy
1.	_____	_____	_____
	_____	_____	_____
2.	_____	_____	_____
	_____	_____	_____
3.	_____	_____	_____
	_____	_____	_____
	_____	_____	_____

Challenge Three: We Operate with a Human Mind. When you think about it, it is as if the gods have played a cosmic joke on us. On the one hand, they have gifted us with a mind that allows us to reflect upon and appreciate every aspect of life. Consider, if you will, the mind's capacity for abstract thought. We can reflect on such things as the nature of truth or beauty, anticipate future events, contemplate our own experiences, be self-aware, apply reason and logic to solve problems, and more. What an advantage this gives us in navigating through life, as opposed to the other creatures with whom we share this planet.

But that's not all. Our human mind also gives us the ability to communicate with people in meaningful ways. We can share information and ideas, work together to solve problems, and collaborate to create what did not previously exist. Perhaps most rewarding, this ability to communicate provides us the foundation for developing interpersonal relationships. After all, what is a relationship if not a repeated pattern of communication between one person's mind and that of another person. Think how pleasurable it is to share our intimate thoughts, feelings, and emotions with others.

Our human mind is also the source of the experience to love. Love is that powerful feeling we have for another person who we fervently believe has and will provide us with exactly what we need to be happy. For example, when I first met my wife, I thought, "She's really neat." Then, after repeated interactions, my evaluative judgments progressed to "She's very special," followed by, "She has what I deeply long for," and then finally, "Having her in my life would make my life happy." As my beliefs about her progressed, so did my value for her. At some point, I came to value her to such a degree that I could honestly say that I loved her. Without our mind, we may have a visceral, animalistic attraction to another, but it takes our mental judgments and evaluations to truly create the experience of love.

As if that wasn't enough, our minds also give us our sense of humor, providing all the ingredients for laughter and mirth. "Did you hear about the depressed dyslexic? He threw himself behind the bus." Why do you chuckle when you hear this joke? Because you conceptually get it. We laugh because we understand irony, absurdity, and contradiction.

Finally, our minds fuel our ability to enjoy a variety of higher-level sensibilities. Only with our abstract mind can we appreciate and find pleasure in paintings, music, opera, ballet, and literature. The same is also true with regard to watching a football, basketball, or baseball game. We can only appreciate these with our conceptual ability to connect what we see and hear to our likes and dislikes.

All of these, and probably many more, are the blessings we derive from our human mind. But here's the punch line. Despite all these gifts with which our human mind graces us, we are not concurrently blessed with the ability to use it consistently well. We find it all too easy to choose fiction over fact, distort reality, pay attention to certain parts of reality while ignoring others, exaggerate degrees of badness, and conclude that a certain outcome is absolutely necessary to our existence when, in fact, it is not. We also tend to judge, evaluate, or label ourselves and others as totally good or bad based on a single behavior or trait.

I see the ravages of this faulty thinking every day in my office. Take, for example, Robert, Joanne, Sara, Joel, and Valerie, each of whom suffer from severe depression due to the false conviction that they are bad and worthless. Or take Miles, who perpetually put himself through hurt and anger because he interprets every slight or frown as an intentional attempt to put him down. Then there's Brett, Tracy, and Stephen who habitually exaggerate the badness of the events in their lives to the point that they find them intolerable.

These distortions and irrationalities are all tricks of our fallible minds.

We are all prone to fall into their clutches. This is the human condition that presents quite a challenge in our quest for happiness. But remember: By being alert to these distortions, and by working hard to both minimize them and maximize their rational alternatives, you can avoid all kinds of unhappy states into which the patients mentioned above fell.

Prompt Three: Identifying Your Negative Thinking. Now is an opportunity for you to personalize this. Identify below what kind of negative thinking you may habitually engage in about yourself, other people, and your life circumstances in general. For each, note the negative impact this thinking has on your happiness and well-being. Then compose a more rational way to think which would get you to reach more positive emotional results.

	Negative Thinking	Negative Impact	Better Alternative
Self			
1.	_____	_____	_____
	_____	_____	_____
2.	_____	_____	_____
	_____	_____	_____
3.	_____	_____	_____
	_____	_____	_____

Others

1. _____   _____   _____

_____   _____   _____

2. _____   _____   _____

_____   _____   _____

3. _____   _____   _____

_____   _____   _____

Life Circumstances

1. _____   _____   _____

_____   _____   _____

2. _____   _____   _____

_____   _____   _____

3. _____   _____   _____

_____   _____   _____

Going Forward

As I've emphasized, we live in a difficult world, amongst imperfect, mistake-prone people, not saints or angels, and operate with a fallible mind. All of these conditions pose a challenge to our happiness.

But fret not. Millions upon millions of people have overcome these challenges. So can you. Think of this chapter as the first step in creating a happy life for yourself. Now that you've identified your happiness challenges, you have a leg up. You can immediately begin to activate the strategies you've identified in the foregoing exercises to bring you some happiness. And you can add to them to your repertoire as you proceed through the succeeding chapters until you eventually create your own comprehensive strategic Happiness Action Plan in Part III of this book.

Notes

2

VISIONING HAPPINESS

One foundation of all successful psychotherapy is an accurate diagnosis. Another is the setting of vivid, attainable goals. Setting goals makes clear the target. It helps in selecting the precise strategies to make the goals a reality. It provides the patient hope and can motivate him or her to make the effort needed to get better. Setting goals can also make clear to the therapist and the patient when mid-course corrections are needed, as well as to when the therapy process has been successfully completed.

I found goal setting to be extremely important with one of my current patients. Now in his mid-fifties, Bobby had never held a job for more than a few months. The problem was his trigger-happy anger. Lacking self-restraint, he felt compelled to confront anybody and everybody at the drop of a hat. He did this not only with people at work, but also with his wife and children, as well as the people he casually encountered in his day-to-day activities. Resistant to all of my interventions, he walked into my office with his head down, his face long, and his shoulders slumped. What follows is our conversation after he had been fired from his third job in under a year.

BOBBY: I've always blamed everyone else for my anger. It was their fault. They provoked me. It's because of them that I acted the way I did.

Dr. G: And now?

BOBBY: Now? Well, I guess I've got to face the fact that I must be doing something wrong. My supervisor told me that everyone in the plant has complained about me.

Dr. G: Wow, Bobby, that's quite a realization. If you can genuinely own your role in your problems, then you've got a real chance to fix what needs to be fixed. Can you tell me what you think you need to fix?

BOBBBY: Yeah, the way I act.

Dr. G: How so?

BOBBY: I fly off the handle at the drop of a hat. I confront people when they don't do what's right, raise my voice, get in their face.

DR. G: Okay. And I gather that those are exactly the kinds of behaviors others find obnoxious and cause you to get fired. Right?

BOBBY: Yes.

DR. G: Okay, so that's your current reality. Now, starting there, can you envision how you'd have to behave in the future so as not to keep irritating people to the point of getting fired?

BOBBY: I guess I'd have to lighten up, relax, keep my nose out of other peoples' business. Just do my job and stop worrying about how they do theirs.

DR. G: You've got it. But that's easier said than done. So, here's the million-dollar question: What do you need to do to be able to do that?

BOBBY: Control my anger.

DR. G: Close, but that's not exactly the best way to frame it. You need to do more than just control your anger, because, once you become angry, there's no controlling it. What you need to do is not make yourself angry to begin with. Do you see the difference between the two?

BOBBY: Yeah, not getting angry to begin with is different from controlling it once it's already there.

DR. G: Exactly! Once you get angry, especially with your lack of restraint, you swing into action within a split second. Boom! Off you go. Right?

BOBBY: Right.

DR. G: So the goal is for you to learn how not to become angry. Now, what would it take for you to do that?

BOBBY: I know what you want me to say.

DR. G: Forget what I want. This is not a debate between you and me. It's your life we're talking about. What's the truth? What do you need to do to not get yourself so self-destructively angry in the future?

BOBBY: Change the way I think.

DR. G: Specifically?

BOBBY: I know, I know – stop demanding that people be perfect, stop damning them when they act stupid or rude, and stop taking everything they do so personal. Live and let live.

DR. G: That's exactly right. You've got to change that perfectionistic, damning way you think about other people in order to give up your anger and keep a job.

Notice the flow of this conversation. It started with Bobby clearly articulating the current reality of his problems. It then moved to him defining how he'd have to act in the future to no longer defeat himself. Finally, it moved to the beginning of a strategic plan to move him from where he is to where he needs to be. This conversation, in brief, followed the same strategic planning process I had led the doctors through as described previously.

The jury is still out on whether or not Bobby will succeed in ridding himself of his anger. As he told me, "The way I'm supposed to think is so opposite to how I've always thought." All I know is that he and I laid the groundwork for a way for him to act so he can find peace of mind. We defined his current reality, articulated the goals he needs to meet, and agreed upon an elegant strategy for him to succeed. We'll see what happens going forward.

Your goal, of course, is happiness. But, to simply say this is not good enough. I want you, the reader, to know, truly know, what happiness looks like, feels like, and smells like. Beyond merely stating that "my goal is to be happy," I want you to lay out a vivid, fully realized vision of what you would experience if you were truly happy.

Below, I present ten gifts that happiness can bestow, each illustrated with a brief case example. As you read along, ask yourself: Do I regularly experience this gift and, if not, would I like to? Beneath each, I present space for you to make a few notes about what this might look like in your life in anticipation of The Happiness Visioning Workshop to follow.

Ten Happiness Gifts

1. Happiness Feels Good

Yes, happiness just out and out feels good. Take Sarah, for example. She suffered an abhorrent childhood – alcoholic parents who physically abused her, a punitive grandmother who lashed out at her for the slightest infraction, an uncle who sexually molested her. She learned young and fast that the world is a dangerous place. Even worse, she came to believe that all of this wouldn't have happened to her if she were worth a dime. As a consequence, Sarah experienced a soul-killing mixture of depression and anxiety most of her adult life.

Sarah was fifty-one when I first counseled her. Over time, and with much work, she began to believe that she was now just as safe from physical abuse as anyone else. Moreover, she came to understand that, even if someone felt disappointed with her, she still retained her dignity. She saw that she was a worthwhile person – no strings attached. As these realizations took hold, Sarah's entire demeanor changed.

On the Monday after Thanksgiving, Sarah walked into my office, smiled, and said: "Guess what? I had a wonderful Thanksgiving. In fact, I've been happy the whole week. The depression, the anxiety, they're all gone. I feel so lighthearted. If this is happiness, I want more of it."

Sarah proves that, when happy, we just plain feel good. Our spirits lift, our world brightens, our outlook improves. We feel hopeful. To paraphrase Erma Bombeck: Happiness is the gift that keeps on giving. Not only do we feel happy, but we feel happy about feeling happy.

Notes:

_____

_____

_____

2. Happiness Is an Antidote to Unhappiness

Every minute you're unhappy, you can't be happy. Conversely, every minute you're happy, you can't be unhappy. This reminds me of Paul. When I first met him, he habitually saw the glass half-empty. His mood bounced between angst, bitterness, and hopelessness. No matter the conversation, he always sprinkled in a few "Life sucks," "Why bother," or "That's just the way it is."

Like the dinner guest that shows up early and leaves a bit too late, pessimism elbows its way into all our minds now and then. For Paul, it took permanent residence. It slouched back on the couch, propped its feet on the coffee table, and made sure happiness felt unwelcome. If Paul experienced a moment of even the slightest pleasure, he dismissed it as meaningless and expected it would be fleeting. He kept his eyes focused on the horizon, but always looked for the next thundercloud that would validate his inner dreariness.

After years of this behavior, Paul's family had seen enough. They could no longer bear watching him swim in circles of unhappiness. They held an intervention and convinced him to seek the kind of professional help that could mend his killjoy outlook.

Being mired in years of such deep, habitual unhappiness, Paul slogged through therapy the first few weeks. But he and I persisted. We worked to correct his negative thinking and build pleasurable activities into each day. And guess what? As he persisted in these efforts, he found that it was nearly impossible to feel unhappy when having fun, feeling pleasure, and staying positive.

"Doc," he said to me one day, "you can't be pregnant and not pregnant, right? Well, you can't be happy and unhappy at the same time either. Unhappiness used to kick out my happiness, but now it's the other way around." He shook his head, amazed at how far he had come, and added. "I want more of it."

We all have our moments of gloom. But in that moment when we feel happy, we cannot also feel unhappy. Positive emotions undid and blocked out Paul's negative emotions. They can do the same for anyone.

Notes:

---

3. Happiness Attracts Others to Us

At first glance you'd predict that Mary would be happy. In her mid-thirties, she lived in a city ripe with culture and entertainment. She owned a small catering business – tasty and successful. She held her own in any intellectual discussion. And, when in the supermarket, she attracted more than a few glances from men.

Yet something didn't add up. She felt lonely and dissatisfied. Connecting with people seemed impossible. Underneath this veneer, Mary carried the blight of self-doubt, accompanied by a crippling fear of rejection. In turn, she became shy, emotionally aloof, and self-absorbed. All that culminated in an attitude that seemed to say, "Leave me alone."

In psychotherapy, Mary worked past these issues. She transformed into someone much more self-accepting, relaxed, and open. She freed herself to crack jokes, act spontaneously around people, and exude openness and interest.

A few weeks later, while grabbing coffee, she noticed the guy behind her in line. They'd said hello a few times before, but nothing beyond that. On a whim, Mary suggested they grab a seat and enjoy their coffee together. And that's what they did – for two hours.

"You know," the guy said on the way out the door, "when I first met you, I was kind of put off. You seemed aloof, arrogant. I couldn't put my finger on it. But was I way off."

Despite the fact that Mary's now dating this man, the lesson here is that feeling happy shows; it simply makes us more attractive to others. Keep this in mind: People remember how you make them feel long after they remember what you say. If you're happy, you're a pleasure to be around.

_____

_____

_____

4. Happiness Contributes to Other's Happiness

Anchored to his senior executive position, Amy's husband Jeff carried such a high level of stress that he often came home morose, grouchy, and impatient. The fun-loving and affectionate man she married no longer seemed there. Fed-up, increasingly bitter, and withdrawn herself, Amy finally told her husband one night that his mood was not only wrecking her own but also destroying the fabric of her love for him. "We need help before we end up in divorce court," she said.

Jeff listened to Amy's concerns. With professional guidance, they both set out on a campaign to decontaminate themselves emotionally. She worked to relinquish her anger. He worked to de-stress himself. He picked up exercising again, cut back on the alcohol, and made sure he got a solid eight hours of sleep each night. Most importantly, he gave up his obsession with success and adjusted his focus to include his family and friends alongside his work. Both Amy and Jeff reclaimed their personal happiness – and that fed straight into their happiness with each other. Her husband once again became the man she married. She, in turn, became the woman with whom he first fell in love. The more happiness Jeff felt and expressed, the more pleasure and happiness Amy experienced – which she returned in spades. And, of course, their connection as a couple deepened. At our last session, Amy smiled and said, "I've got my husband back."

The bottom line is that family, friends, associates, and even strangers you encounter all benefit from your happiness, just as you benefit from theirs. Everyone wins when you're happy.

Notes:

_____

_____

_____

5. Happiness Enlivens and Sharpens Our Minds

A myth that pervades many artistic circles is that a person needs to live a life of suffering and misery in order to create something of universal beauty. Put on the pedestal as a role model is the hard-drinking writer, the brooding actor, the painter, or the sculptor who can only exorcise his or her demons through work.

This, of course, is utter claptrap. Think what it would do to your energy if you had to lug a fifty-pound weight around all day. Think how poorly you'd perform at your job if deprived of sleep for nights on end.

The truth is that your mind never works better than when you're happy. You're focused and alert, your concentration is sharp, you are a better problem solver, you thrive on ideas, and you are open to new concepts and experiences. Your creativity skyrockets along with your intellectual engagement. You have more mental resources to draw upon each day, which can open doors you never knew existed.

Take a look at one of the experiments Martin Seligman reported in his groundbreaking book, *Authentic Happiness* (2002). Researchers randomly placed forty-four doctors into one of three groups: They gave one group candy; they assigned a second group the task of reading positive statements about medicine; and they gave nothing at all to a third group. All forty-four physicians were then asked to think out loud as they diagnosed a difficult liver disease case. The first and second groups performed the best – they considered liver disease earlier and arrived at the correct diagnosis much faster than group three.

A happy mood enlivens our mind – and this creates a perpetuating circle. Happiness gives us good ideas; good ideas give us new and better solutions to problems; and successful problem solving gives us increased satisfaction and happiness.

Notes:

_____

_____

_____

6. Happiness Enhances Our Health

I have a friend I hesitate to call a senior citizen, although he recently turned eighty. He perfectly fits the ancient Greek saying: "A happy mind in a happy body."

Rick always greets me with a hearty hello, a firm handshake, even a bear hug. He exudes confidence but not arrogance, optimism but not pollyannaism, goodwill without self-sacrifice. His wife says he's even like that at home.

And Rick's more physically fit than most thirty-year-olds I know. Sure, once he hit seventy, he traded in 10k's for 5k's, he goes to bed at 10:00 rather than 11:30, and he now lifts weights only three times a week. But look past all that. The happier Rick feels, the healthier he feels, and vice-versa.

But Rick's is not a unique case. Research shows that happiness is a prime contributor to physical health. Happy people live longer, they experience fewer disabilities, catch fewer colds, and have lower blood pressure. Furthermore, happy people take much better care of themselves than their less happy brethren; they exercise more, act proactively with health risk information, and regularly take advantage of medical expertise. All that adds up to another old saying: "It is not the years in our life that count, but the life in our years."

Notes:

_____

_____

_____

7. Happiness Promotes Productivity

Years before, Bill had published four books of poetry and painted oils that he sold in exhibits throughout the Southeast. He did all that while conducting a successful graphic artist career.

But all that was long ago, before depression entered his life and wrecked both his mood and his motivation, not to mention his creativity. It didn't take long to uncover the causes of his depression. He not only considered himself a total loser because of two failed marriages that separated him from his three children, but he also catastrophized that his future was irrevocably hopeless. Harboring these two spirit-killing beliefs, it was little wonder that he dragged himself to his day job and flopped on the couch when off work.

Bill made good use of his therapy. After a few fits and starts, he actively challenged his negative beliefs about both himself and his future. As his depression lifted, his zest gradually returned. It wasn't long thereafter that he decided to develop a cartoon series that highlighted both his visual and his verbal artistic skills.

You see, unhappy people carry dissatisfaction about today and worry about tomorrow. They suffer depression about themselves and their lives. They focus on performing to perfection and having their desires satisfied. And they harbor anger and resentment toward the difficult people and circumstances they encounter. You guessed it – they are so focused on what's wrong in their lives that they eliminate the possibility for problem solving, productivity, and, yes, creativity.

Happy people, conversely, are neither anxious nor depressed. Not obsessively focused on getting what they want, they strive to do well but are satisfied with less than perfection. They do not ruminate about past or present injustices. Instead, they spend their days in the company of a strong, content peace of mind.

If you need a compelling argument to seek happiness, look no further. Unburdened by unhappiness, happy people find it easy to focus on their chores and tasks, put more energy into and perform better at work, and still find time to complete hobbies and avocations. And, as you can imagine, they report more job satisfaction than their unhappy brethren.

So it's as simple as this: The happier you feel, the more you can accomplish.

Notes:

_____

_____

_____

8. Happiness Builds Emotional Resilience

Now and then, life serves all of us lemons. Sometimes these are minor – a leaky faucet, a sprained ankle, a dented fender. Other times they rise to the level of genuine hardship: A major illness, losing a loved one, a financial crisis. To be sure, happiness provides an edge, not only when surviving these challenges, but recovering from them as well.

Nobody had more of a challenge than Gail. Within a year, she lost her mother to cancer and her father to a heart attack. After an understandable – and needed – period of mourning, she amazingly bounced backed from these tragedies. She regained a zest for life, a sense of humor, and a passion for friends and work.

What was the secret to Gail's recovery? During several lengthy interviews, I learned that she had committed to a set of five mindsets, adopted over a lifetime.

With Gail's permission, I pass them on to you: (1) she steadfastly looked toward the future with a sense of hope; (2) she strove to unconditionally accept herself; (3) she believed that her life had purpose and meaning; (4) she made sure to be grateful for life's blessings; and (5) she approached the people in her life with a non-judgmental, forgiving attitude.

These mindsets are critical to happiness. Unbeknownst to Gail, these mindsets not only brought her happiness but they also prepared her to bounce back from her twin tragedies.

We all know what medical doctors tell us: Exercise, diet, and rest build a strong immune system to help us ward off the flu. Happiness is the same: Today's peace of mind prepares us for tomorrow's adversity.

Notes:

_____

_____

_____

9. Happiness Spawns Openheartedness

During a television interview a number of years ago, the actor Richard Gere told a story about a period before he became a recognizable celebrity. For two whole days, with his heart filled with happiness, he walked the streets of notoriously impersonal New York City and directed the thought, "I love you," to each person he passed on the street. To his amazement, Gere observed two results: first, he experienced even more happiness himself and, second, though he never smiled, nodded, or spoke, strangers who passed smiled at him.

The lesson Gere teaches us is that the happier you are, the more you open your heart. Happiness spawns a loving and positive frame of mind. And, as a result, you become more emotionally giving and show more kind, generous, and empathic behavior. You get back what you give.

Notes:

_____

_____

_____

10. Happiness Makes Us Playful

Nothing Bryan did was good enough – or so his parents and teachers told him. They let him know that he needed to be perfect: Stop this, change that, do the other better. So Bryan set out to become a saint. Naturally, he couldn't quite achieve that lofty ambition, but that didn't prevent him from trying. His somber childhood led to a somber adulthood. Every task became a matter of life or death. If he failed, guilt and shame weighed on his shoulders for weeks. Eventually, he began to dread each day.

In time, Bryan realized that he had a problem and came by my office. I first helped him appreciate how debilitating his drive for perfection was. Then I encouraged him to refute the perfectionistic ambitions that drove his life. Finally, I talked him off the ledge of sainthood onto more reasonable, human ground. Through this process, he developed a new philosophy: "I'm a fallible human and can't be perfect. My worth as a person doesn't depend on how I perform a task. I'll do my best. That's all I can do. So I'm just going to relax and enjoy the ride."

The fog of Bryan's anxiety, shame, and depression lifted. When he did something well, he felt proud, but, when he didn't, he regretted it without self-damning. By eliminating his perfectionism, and divorcing his personal worth from his performance, he noticed he could enjoy simply doing.

In the process of making these profound changes, Bryan became a light-hearted young man. He discovered that he held a wry sense of humor. He developed friendships and interests with the same zeal that he pursued career success. He took up tennis and found pleasure in both the exercise and the friendships he made on the court. He built more fun into his life and found himself living with more zest. So, happiness can make you more playful as well.

Notes:

_____

_____

_____

The Happiness Visioning Workshop

Now it's time for you to get back to work. This Happiness Visioning Workshop is the second step in creating your happy life. Along with the picture of the current reality you drew in Chapter 1, this vision can help you make your strategic happiness choices in Chapters 4–8. So, again, with courage, hopefulness, and commitment, please respond thoughtfully to the following three prompts.

Prompt One: My Current Reality. What follows is a list of the ten happiness gifts discussed before. For each, check the degree to which they describe you: Always, Often, Sometimes, Rarely, or Never. As you do this, be honest, because those which you rate low can be strengthened. They will give you direction as you develop your Happiness Action Plan down the road. As you reflect on these, again note any helpful ideas you may have to help you feel happiness.

	Always	Often	Sometimes	Rarely	Never
1. Happiness feels good.	_____	_____	_____	_____	_____

Notes:

_____

_____

_____

	Always	Often	Sometimes	Rarely	Never
2. Happiness is an antidote to unhappiness.	_____	_____	_____	_____	_____

Notes:

_____

_____

_____

	Always	Often	Sometimes	Rarely	Never
3. Happiness attracts others to us.	_____	_____	_____	_____	_____

Notes:

_____

_____

_____

4. Happiness contributes to other's happiness.

_____ _____ _____ _____ _____

Notes:

_____

_____

_____

5. Happiness enlivens and sharpens our minds.

_____ _____ _____ _____ _____

Notes:

_____

_____

_____

6. Happiness enhances our health.

_____ _____ _____ _____ _____

Notes:

_____

_____

_____

7. Happiness promotes productivity.

_____ _____ _____ _____ _____

Notes:

_____

_____

_____

8. Happiness builds emotional _____ _____ _____ _____ _____
resilience.

Notes:

_____

_____

_____

9. Happiness spawns _____ _____ _____ _____ _____
openheartedness.

Notes:

_____

_____

_____

10. Happiness makes us playful. _____ _____ _____ _____ _____

Notes:

_____

_____

_____

Prompt Two: Thinking Ahead. Now that you have a picture of where you stand on the gifts that make for a happy life, you can begin to envision your future happiness. For those you rated Sometimes, Rarely, or Never, make a list of the benefits that would be yours if they rated Always or Often. Then note one or two actions you could immediately take to improve these ratings. In doing this, don't forget to maintain your confidence and sense of hope.

	Happiness Gift	My Benefit	Immediate Action
1.	_____	_____	_____
	_____	_____	_____
2.	_____	_____	_____
	_____	_____	_____

3. _____   _____   _____

_____   _____   _____

4. _____   _____   _____

_____   _____   _____

5. _____   _____   _____

_____   _____   _____

Prompt Three: My Happiness Vision. Building on these two prompts, now describe what a happy life would look and feel like to you. To give you an example, consider the Happiness Vision I created for myself:

> To build and sustain a life that frees me to only do the things that provide excitement, pleasure, and satisfaction, that creates an amount of income that makes money a non-issue, that balances fulfilling work with family and recreational time, and that promotes my life's purpose.

As you create your own Happiness Vision below, let your imagination flow. It's yours to create as you wish. In your own words, describe what a happy life would look and feel like to you. Paint as vivid a picture as you can, neither holding back nor playing it safe. Be as syrupy as you want. Describe what and whom it would include. Remember: This is the future Vision you will attempt to make real through your Happiness Action Plan brainstormed in Part II and pulled together in Part III.

My Happiness Vision

Going Forward

Both the definition of your current happiness reality and the vision of the happy future you desire sets the stage for the finalization of your comprehensive Happiness Action Plan that comes later. The next chapter, "Chapter 3: The Happiness Mindsets," starts you on the path to lifelong happiness. It provides you with five mental perspectives that, if consciously and energetically adopted, will empower you to create enduring happiness. Please pay careful attention to and consider adopting these principles as your own.

Notes

_____
_____
_____
_____
_____
_____
_____
_____
_____
_____
_____
_____
_____
_____
_____
_____
_____
_____
_____
_____
_____
_____
_____
_____
_____
_____
_____
_____
_____
_____
_____
_____
_____

3

THE HAPPINESS MINDSETS

You have now identified in Chapter 1 the forces that are aligned against you in your search for happiness. You have also crafted in Chapter 2 a vision of what you want your life to look like once you find it. Now comes the first step in your strategic action plan – deciding to adopt those mindsets necessary for you to build a life filled with happiness. The decisions you make with regard to these will have a profound impact on the lengths you will go to secure it. Be thoughtful as you digest them and consider adopting them as your own.

The following five mindsets, then, provide the leverage you need to avidly pursue your happiness. They can fuel your sustained use of the practices that I will lay out in Part II of *The Serious Business of Being Happy*. Read them, absorb them, and consider adopting them as your happiness foundation.

Mindset One: This Is It

There is an old joke about a man walking along the roof of a fifty-story building who trips and falls over the edge. As he falls past the twenty-seventh floor, someone inside calls out, "How's it going?" The falling man says, "So far, so good."

Of course, we all know what's coming – a splat on the pavement. Sooner or later, all of us will hit the pavement. Perhaps that's what triggers uncomfortable chuckles when I tell this joke. Death is the destination all of us share.

But, strange as it may sound, that realization can provide you with a great source of happiness. It's a stark reminder that, yes, this is it. Today is all we have. Tomorrow might be no different or better. Besides, none of us know for certain that there will even be a tomorrow.

That's exactly the lesson Robert learned in his quest to find happiness. Depressed after retiring from his job as a hospital administrator, he retreated to the couch in his den where he spent pretty much all day every day. With nothing productive to do, he fell into the habit of brooding about how useless he was and how bland his life had become.

After his wife half-seriously said, "I don't know whether to shoot you or myself," Robert sought out psychotherapy. Once he turned around his negative thinking, he remarked, "You know, I've only got a certain number of years left, so what the hell am I doing wasting my precious time?" With that, he got off his duff. He signed up for adult continuing education classes, booked a second honeymoon Caribbean cruise with his wife, and started dabbling in watercolor painting. No more dawdling for him. Along with his newfound positive attitude and commitment to stimulating activities came a wealth of pleasure and, yes, happiness.

Many of us take living for granted. There will always be tomorrow. There will always be the next day, the next, and then the next. But can't that attitude easily lead to complacency, drifting, even wasting our precious time? If we keep in mind that our time on earth is limited, then we can consciously and intentionally seek happiness every day – one day at a time.

Prompt One: Applying "This Is It." The bottom line: There are precious few days in your life. Remember that as often as possible. That perspective will help you consciously and intentionally seek happiness at every turn. To live according to "This is it," try to:

- Become increasingly aware of what does and does not bring happiness to your life;
- Focus on the opportunities that exist each day to experience happiness;
- Purposely build into your life – step by step – those things that give you happiness;
- Systematically rid your life – little by little – of those things that bring frustration, displeasure, and suffering;
- Be grateful for and savor those moments of happiness already experienced, thereby prolonging the original experiences themselves.

Before continuing onto the second source of happiness, take a few minutes to list three things that you could immediately integrate into your daily life to increase your pleasure quotient.

1.

_____

2.

_____

3.

_____

Mindset Two: If It's Going To Be, It's Up To Me

Nobody is put on this earth to make sure you are happy. Maybe your parents had some responsibility early on. After all, they brought you into this world without your permission. But their job ended long ago. Neither does your happiness rest on the shoulders of your significant other, your children, your friends, your employer, or your community. It's up to you. Entirely.

This can be a hard pill to swallow. We all know people like Alexis, who devoted years of her life steeped in bitterness because her husband of fifteen years walked out on her. We all know someone like John, who still rails against his parents because they never showed him the warmth or love he wanted. And, of course there's Beth, who dwelled on the inequities she faced as she tried to climb the corporate ladder.

Each of these people wallowed in a toxic mix of bitterness and self-pity that blocked any possibility of happiness. Life was unfair, they declared. People and conditions should be different than they were. It was damned awful to have to live in such a god-awful world as this. This was their mindset and, according to them, things would have to change "out there" for them to be happy.

It took all the persistence I could muster to wrangle Alexis, John, and Beth out of their victim mentality and into a take-charge one. Once they accepted that, their therapy yielded two bounties. The first was relief from their spirit-killing bitterness; the second was the emotional freedom to pursue happiness.

Thankfully, these three people finally achieved the happiness they desired. And so can you, but only if you embrace the fact that your happiness is your responsibility – 100%. It is your job entirely. If the universe happens to cooperate, see it as a bonus.

Prompt Two: Accepting Personal Responsibility. To live by Mindset Two: If It's Going To Be, It's Up To Me, you will want to consider adopting the following guidelines:

- Gracefully accept that life will throw you curves along the path of your pursuit of happiness;
- Be resolute in working to overcome those adversities that challenge your quest for happiness;
- Refuse to fall into the victim mentality when things do not go your way, not giving in to whining, self-pitying, and blaming;
- Be absolutely determined to take charge of filling as many moments as possible in your life with happiness;

- Adopt the Serenity Prayer: God grant me the wisdom to accept the things I cannot change, the courage to change the things I can, and the wisdom to know the difference.

Now, thoughtfully address the following three questions. They are not inconsequential. Take your time. Be honest with yourself. Your answers do matter with regard to your future happiness:

(1) Where, when, and under what circumstances do you fall into the trap of expecting others to look out for your happiness?

_____

_____

(2) What negative consequences do you suffer when you fall prey to this type of thinking – emotionally? behaviorally? interpersonally?

_____

_____

(3) What specifically will you do to step up to the plate and either change the unwanted circumstances or gracefully lump them?

_____

_____

Mindset Three: Decide To Be Happy

Think of the major decisions you've made that have profoundly affected your life – the college in which you decided to enroll; the mate you chose to marry; where you decided to live; whether or not to have children; your career direction. The odds are that the ripples of these decisions are still visible. They were moments of truth from which the entire trajectory of your life sprang.

Here's another decision to add to that inventory: Should I decide to be happy? I'll bet that you've never sat down and made that decision. But what if you consciously and resolutely did so? Wouldn't that spur you to take action to make this decision a reality?

This decision proved to be the cherry on top of the sundae for sixty-four-year-old Mark. A civil engineer, he reported a lifetime of depression and anxiety, precipitated by a cold and cruel mother who threatened and criticized him throughout his childhood. "I've spent my early life looking over my shoulder for fear that I'd be erased by her," he said.

But that wasn't what spurred Mark to seek my help. It was an escalation of anxiety after his wife physically attacked him. In my opinion, this sorry incident proved to be a blessing in disguise, as it opened the door for him to address the trauma he experienced in his youth.

As I typically do, I applied the techniques of Rational Emotive Behavior Therapy to Mark. Slowly but surely he identified and relinquished the irrational beliefs that caused his unhappiness – the assumption that he was in constant danger; the conviction that disapproval or annoyance would be so horrible he couldn't bear it; the belief that he was a pitiful, worthless person who must have deserved what he got. As he did so, his depression and anxiety lightened.

One day, he settled onto my office couch and said, "I feel so less emotionally burdened, but is this all I can hope for, just relief from my unhappiness?" *Great question*, I thought, and then I engaged him in the conversation that follows...

DR. G: Well what would you want now that you've got rid of your misery?

MARK: I don't know.

DR. G.: Well, how about happiness?

MARK: Happiness? What's that? I don't think I've ever felt that – ever! How in the world would I ever make that happen?

DR. G.: Well, it starts with your deciding that you're going to be happy. What if you made a flat out, full-blown commitment to make yourself happy?

MARK: That's it? That'll do it for me?

DR. G.: Of course not, but to put the needed effort into bringing happiness into your life, it would sure help for you to make a firm, heartfelt decision that that's what you're going to do – be happy. After that comes the strategic plan, which I'll help you create, if you want. Make sense?

MARK: Yes.

DR. G.: Well?

MARK: Okay, I'm in. I'll fully commit to bring happiness into my life.

DR. G: All right! So, let's start the plan.

Mark worked as hard on bringing happiness into his life as he did to conquer his depression and anxiety. It started with his committed decision to be happy. And the same can happen with you.

Prompt Three: Your Happiness Decision. Determine to do whatever is necessary to bring yourself daily happiness. Commit to seek happiness throughout your life. Once you do, you can, thoughtfully and with clear purpose, take these steps:

- Remind yourself each morning that this day is an opportunity to be happy;
- Earmark daily those people and activities you enjoy;
- Pay conscious attention to savoring each and every moment you experience pleasure;

- Make sure that the things you find most important do not take a backseat to things you find of lesser importance;
- Fervently teach the value of happiness to your loved ones.

Before going on, please ponder these pivotal questions about your quest for happiness:

1. What benefits will you derive from deciding to make happiness a central goal in your life?

_____

_____

2. What will the benefits be to your loved ones, close friends, and community by deciding to be happy?

_____

_____

Mindset Four: Attitude Is Everything

Literally thousands of research studies have taught us something remarkable about human nature. It is that neither our happiness nor our unhappiness comes from the outside circumstances in our lives. Rather, they come from the way we think about those circumstances. In Rational Emotive Behavior Therapy (REBT), we illustrate this through the now-famous ABC model (see Figure 3.1).

In this model, A represents the *Activating Event*, that is, the people, places, and things about which we react with either happiness or unhappiness. C represents the *Consequence*, the emotional, behavioral, and/or physiological reaction we have to the event – happy or unhappy. Contrary to other therapies, REBT asserts that it is not the A that causes the C, but the B, the *Belief*, which mediates between A and C. In other words, we author our own happiness or unhappiness in response to the events we encounter in our lives by the way we think about them.

By way of example, take three people – Jack, Jeff, and Joe. Each got a speeding ticket on their way to work. Although they faced the same Activating Event (the A), they each experienced different emotional consequences (the C) – Jack felt guilt and shame, Jeff anger, and Joe magnanimity and grace. These three

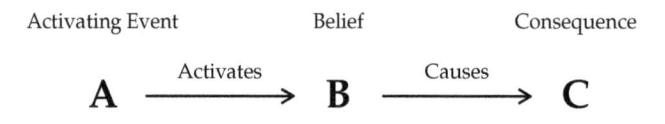

Figure 3.1 REBT's ABC Model

gentlemen reacted so differently because they each cognitively processed their speeding ticket (the B) in radically different ways:

JACK: "I should have been more careful. I can't do anything right. What a loser I am."

JEFF: "Who the hell does that cop think he is, lurking in the shadows, waiting to stick it to law-abiding citizens like me? I'd like to punch his &*%$ lights out."

JOE: "Oh, well, I guess I made a mistake, but I'm human and can learn from it."

Notice again that Jack, Jeff, and Joe confronted the same Activating Event at A, but they each experienced different consequences at C. Why? Because they cognitively processed their experience quite differently at B. How they each framed the event determined the exact way that they each reacted.

To say it another way, the responsibility for how Jack, Jeff, and Joe each reacted fell squarely on their respective shoulders. While they may not always have a hand in what they encountered in their lives, they were always responsible for how they reacted to it. If you think about it, this is quite empowering. By acknowledging their responsibility for how they reacted, they could work to react differently in the future by intentionally altering the way they think. So can you.

Now, let's go one step deeper. When we consider the B (the Belief), there are Bs and then there are Bs. Some are more concrete and situation-specific, while others are more abstract and generalized across situations. As shown in Figure 3.2, they can be contextualized, reciprocal, and interactive.

Notice that this figure identifies three varieties of beliefs. At the most concrete and conscious level are the specific thoughts (B_t) that a person has about a particular event (the A). For Jack, for example, his belief was: "I should've been more careful. What a loser I am. I can't do anything right." This thought

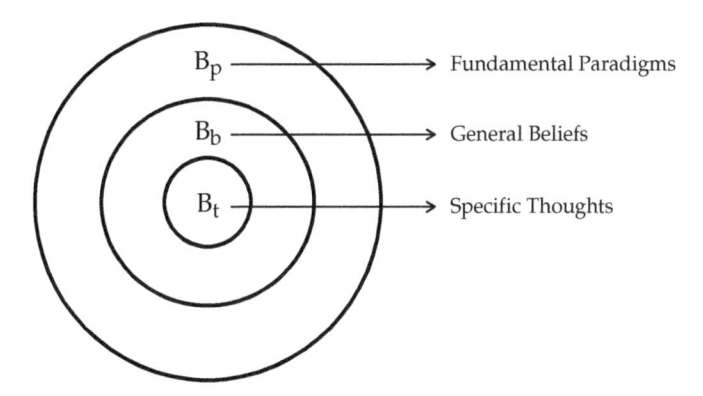

Figure 3.2 The Contextualized ABC Model

by itself would be sufficient to cause him shame and guilt and, therefore, be worthy of therapeutic attention.

But most often these situationally-specific thoughts are influenced by the more general beliefs one holds about oneself, others, and/or life in general. Jack, for instance, might very well hold a perfectionistic belief that he imposes on himself across all situations: "I should never make a mistake." Such a general belief would predictably prompt him to think exactly as he did in that particular situation. We REBT therapists would not only want to help Jack change the way he thought about that particular Activating Event but, more importantly, want to help eliminate his more fundamental perfectionistic belief as well.

Yet there is an even more overarching type of belief which REBTers call a paradigm – a B_p. Paradigms set the context in which the beliefs (the B_b) are held, which in turn influence the situationally-specific ways one thinks (the B_t). For example, Jack's paradigm would first be that there is an absolute law of the universe that commands perfect performance of people and, furthermore, that it is possible to judge a person in his or her entirety as all good or bad.

In REBT, we strive for elegance. By that, I mean we not only want to correct faulty situationally-specific thinking at B_t, but we also want to do away with dysfunctional beliefs (B_b) and paradigms (B_p) as well. Without ridding these more general Bs, it becomes next to impossible to think rationally in specific situations. Looking ahead, this book will offer you happiness-inducing beliefs (B_b) and paradigms (B_p) for you to adopt about yourself, others, and life in general so as to give you the best chance to experience regular and sustained happiness.

Prompt Four: Attitude Adjustment. Attitude is indeed everything. You may possess all the trappings of happiness – health, money, physical attractiveness, power, status – but you will cripple your ability to be happy with a negative frame of mind. In contrast, you may be deprived of most all worldly niceties but still be happy with a good attitude. Your attitude isn't just important; it's crucial.

Every day I'm in my clinical office, I help people shed their happiness-destroying beliefs in favor of ones that promote happiness, despite the presence of annoying circumstances in their lives.

Similarly, each of us can purposely create both happiness and unhappiness with our state of mind. We can train our minds to focus on a beneficial way of thinking, whatever our circumstances. After all, it is not the circumstances but the meaning that we take from them that counts.

Part II of this book, The Happiness Practices, addresses, among other things, those attitudes that give you the best chance of creating happiness in your life. To set the stage, you will want to:

- Accept that you largely control your own emotional state by the beliefs you hold;
- Become a keen observer of your own thinking, so that you can quickly spot those thoughts and beliefs that undercut your happiness;
- Actively convince yourself how irrational and self-defeating are those beliefs that crush your happiness;
- Determine exactly what beliefs you need to experience frequent and regular happiness (make a list and post it in a prominent place as a reminder is not a bad idea);
- Review your happiness-producing beliefs on a daily basis to keep them alive and active.

Now, answer the following two questions:

(1) What would be the benefits to you of accepting emotional responsibility for your mood? What would be the profound drawbacks of refusing to accept this responsibility?

_____

_____

(2) List three slogans or mantras that you can adopt. Think of something like "Life is good" or "Don't worry, be happy."

_____

_____

Mindset Five: Work, Work, Work

Simply hoping and praying that you'll experience happiness without effort is foolhardy. You need to work, work, and then work some more at it. Take this book. I didn't write it in one fell swoop. I took many months to get it just the way I wanted it. Chapter by chapter, I wrote a first draft, revised it, then revised it again. Then, once I finished the last chapter, I combed through the whole thing once more to try to make it even better. The same is true with creating happiness – it isn't a one-time job. You must keep at it, one day at a time, for the rest of your life.

Sound daunting? Well, that unfortunately is the way it is. Look at it logically: If you devote just half an hour to working on your happiness every day, you will give yourself a leg-up on being happy the remaining twenty-three and one-half hours. Quite a bargain.

Fifty-two-year-old Lisa is the poster child for a patient willing to work, work, work. Wracked with depression, anxiety, and guilt as a result of the verbal, physical, and sexual abuse that she suffered throughout her childhood, she had undergone four inpatient hospitalizations and three bouts of electroshock therapy.

Lisa initially floundered in therapy, believing that unhappiness was her lot. Finally, after persistent cajoling on my part, she agreed to start off each day with thirty minutes of hard, persistent work on correcting her self-hating beliefs until more positive ones would take hold in her mind. Her breakthrough came when she remarked to her husband the week of Christmas, "I'm almost afraid to say this, but I feel happy."

So, the bad news is: You must work, work, work to be happy. But the good news is: The work will pay off.

Prompt Five: Getting to Work. With all this in mind, I strongly urge you to:

- Acknowledge the fact that happiness will not be presented to you on a silver platter, and accept that you will need to put in the effort required;
- Take the time to thoughtfully develop your Happiness Action Plan (Chapter 9), picking the strategies most cogent to you from what is to immediately follow in Part II (Chapters 4–8).
- Overcome your tendency to run away from hard work by irrationally thinking the effort is too hard. Remember: A little effort on the front end has the potential for tons of happiness on the back end;
- Strive each and every day to integrate the happiness attitudes and practices to follow in Chapters 4–8 into the fabric of your life;
- Keep working to implement your Happiness Action Plan over the long haul, and resist feeling discouraged by those days that you fail to feel happy. In other words, don't seek perfection with regard to your happiness.

So, here are two reflective questions for you to ponder. How you answer these questions will determine the degree to which you will do what's necessary to make you happy:

(1) List the two most common roadblocks (e.g., bad attitude, busy schedule) that impede your working toward your happiness.

_____

_____

(2) What can you do to overcome these roadblocks?

_____

_____

Going Forward

Thus far, you have laid out the foundation upon which to build the happiness you desire. You understand the difficult challenges you face in bringing yourself happiness. You can envision what a happy life would look like for you. And you can define the five mindsets you must adopt to become happy.

Now is the time to move on to The Happiness Practices. Roll up your sleeves, grab a pencil to make notes, and get to work. Carefully study these practices. Embrace those that you find useful. Decide which ones you will include in your Happiness Action Plan. Those practices that you fervently adopt will determine the degree of happiness you experience the rest of your life.

Notes

PART II

THE HAPPINESS PRACTICES

Part II: The Happiness Practices is where the rubber hits the road. It is the section of *The Serious Business of Being Happy* where you can select the exact paradigms, perspectives, and practices that will help you create the happy life I know you want.

The five chapters in Part II address the three critical elements of the definition of happiness I presented in this book's Introduction. As you will recall, I defined happiness as:

1. *"Acting in accordance with your passionate purpose...."* This is the thrust of Chapter 4: "Live Your Passionate Purpose," the chapter in which you will have an opportunity to create your life's purpose and be shown how to integrate it throughout the fabric of your life.
2. *"Grounded in rational thought about yourself, other people, and life in general...."* Chapters 5: "Happiness With Yourself," 6: "Happiness With Others", and 7: "Happiness With Life" each provide profound cognitive paradigms and behavioral strategies you can adopt to do just that – create happiness with yourself, others, and the circumstances in your life. You can use strategies from all three of these chapters that you determine will be most relevant to your future happiness.
3. *"And guided by your sacred principles...."* Character counts. In Chapter 8: "Live Your Sacred Principles," you will also be given an opportunity to craft the ethical principles you will use to guide your behavior as your pursue your passionate purpose and act to bring about happiness with regard to yourself, others in your life, and your life circumstances in general.

An ambitious agenda I set out for you in Part II, wouldn't you agree? Each of these five chapters stand independently on their own, so you can work through them in sequence or hop around as you wish. They each first offer what I call a

Breakthrough Strategy, a strategy that is powerfully valuable in and of itself, but one that opens the door to those that follow. Then I provide several additional powerful cognitive and behavioral strategies. Study them, absorb them, determine which you think will be of the most use to you. Also, note that there is a page at the end of each chapter for you to organize your thoughts. Don't ignore this opportunity to jot down important ideas and strategies that can help you later.

One last bit of advice before you sink your teeth into Part II. Be as inclusive as you can in noting strategies you can use for your happiness. Don't hold back. Select as many in each chapter that you might find beneficial. You will have an opportunity to pare that list down to a workable number as you craft your final plan in Part III: Your Happiness Action Plan.

4

LIVE YOUR PASSIONATE PURPOSE[1]

I recently ran into Dave while visiting a mutual friend of ours suffering from a terminal illness. Walking to our cars afterward, I asked him how his retirement was going.

"Not well," he responded through pursed lips.

After I voiced my regret, Dave went on to say: "I don't know what to do with myself. I struggle every day to find something to do. Fighting boredom is tough."

How sad. Dave lived his retirement life without any overarching design or purpose. He clearly experienced very little happiness or satisfaction, much less fulfillment and joy.

By contrast, let me share a personal experience I had some years ago that transformed my life. Back then, I had my professional life by the tail. My clinical practice bulged, companies regularly requested my organizational consulting services, my students at the University of Virginia gave me positive feedback. Yet I still felt frustrated and unfulfilled. Why? It was because I wanted to be a big fish in a big pond, not just a regular fish in a small pond. I wanted to be Tony Robbins, Albert Ellis, and Stephen Covey all wrapped up in one glorious package called me.

Not being one to sit and whine, I hired a professional coach to help me get to the promised land. Margaret and I met by phone for forty-five minutes every other week. In our second conversation, she asked me a question that eventually led to my salvation: "What's unique about you?"

I pondered this for a minute before finally saying: "Nothing, really. I do have talents, but nothing unique, nothing that no one else has or does."

"Bulls_ _t," she practically screamed over the phone. "Until you can clearly see your uniqueness, you'll never get to where you want to be." She then gave me the assignment to ask six people who knew me well what they found unique about me.

The very next day I did so, although I didn't expect anything eye-opening to come of it. The first five promised a thoughtful response within a week. The sixth, Jim, said he didn't need a week. He told me to get a pencil and a piece of paper to write down exactly what he had to say.

This is what he said: "What's unique about you is that you help people make their lives perfect, as they want it. You never deviate from that."

I sat stunned. Jim had nailed it. I would never have been able to articulate that sentiment on my own – not in a year, not in one hundred years. Although I knew I often fell short of it, that was exactly what I had been trying to do with everyone with whom I worked without realizing it. That was what was unique about me. That was my passionate purpose.

And that realization changed my life. I shifted my focus from becoming the next international guru to living out my purpose with all the people I already interacted with – my patients, consultees, and students; my loved ones; my friends and colleagues; whomever I encountered. Starting from that moment, I consciously focused my attention on helping people make their lives perfect, as they wanted them to be. As I did, I felt a dramatic resurgence of energy. My productivity dramatically shot up. I felt a deep sense of satisfaction and fulfillment. In short, I felt happy.

All that's what I want for you too – a happy mix of passion, satisfaction, and fulfillment, not just now and then, but most every day. It starts with you creating the breakthrough strategy of your Passionate Purpose that will guide your life choices. With that in mind, please take whatever time necessary to complete the following workshop.

Breakthrough Strategy One: Passionate Purpose

To help you make the most of this workshop, I want to ground you with three perspectives. They are as follows.

1. The Passionate Purpose Workshop is not a process of discovering, but one of creating. Discovering is about finding life's purpose, which is predetermined for you. It already exists, and your responsibility is to figure out what it is. The problem with this approach is that you have to take it on faith that you indeed have a predetermined purpose. Furthermore, it can be disempowering in the sense that someone or something else has defined your purpose for you.

Much like being in an arranged marriage, you must live it whether you like it or not. Most troublesome is that you can easily become discouraged and even self-deprecating if you fail to figure out what this preordained purpose is.

To the contrary, creating is about determining for yourself what your life's purpose is. You have no predetermined purpose, nor is there a right or wrong one for you. You declare what your purpose is by what speaks to you, excites you, drives you. It is yours to create. It is for no one else but you in order to produce the happiness you want in life.

2. In completing this workshop, be sure to distinguish between goals and purpose. As illustrated in Figure 4.1, goals refer to specific outcomes you want to accomplish. For example, some of my goals are to be physically healthy, participate in a happy intimate relationship, eventually have an enjoyable and adventurous retirement. Consider these to be the "whats" of your life.

Striving to achieve your goals can be very rewarding. However, it is when you can connect your goals to the passionate why behind your goal that you can truly experience happiness. That is what I experience when I consciously connect working with my patients, hanging out with my wife, and mentoring my children to my purpose of helping them make their lives perfect, as they want it to be. Beyond the "what," this is the "why" of life.

3. Lastly, the Passionate Purpose Workshop is a three-step process modeled on Stephen Covey's Private Victory paradigm (1989): (1) reflect on your purpose; (2) create your purpose; (3) live your purpose throughout the fabric of your life. Now let's get to it.

Prompt One: Reflect on Your Purpose. Thoughtfully ponder the following five questions. They provide a basis for getting in touch with your deepest, most cherished values, principles, and desires. They can spawn the material for creating your life's purpose. For each, I will cite its source, explain how it is significant to developing your purpose, and illustrate it with examples from my own experiences.

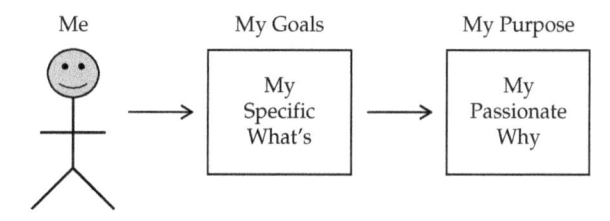

Figure 4.1 Goals and Purpose in Happiness

1. What Am I Doing When I Am in the Flow?

"Flow" is a term coined by the eminent psychiatrist Mihaly Csikszentmihalyi. As described in his seminal book, *Flow* (1991), it refers to a state in which you are so focused on what you are doing that everything else but what you are doing disappears. Time seems to stand still. You are totally absorbed. What you are doing seems effortless and rewarding. When in the "flow," you are most likely engaged in an activity that has deep personal significance to you.

I can identify three activities in my life in which I experienced "flow." When I was younger, I played high school and college basketball. I remember being so absorbed in playing the game that the spectators, coaches, and the outer world often seemed to disappear. In this state, the court, the basketball, and even the other players seemed to be mere pawns for my creative expression.

In my current life, I frequently experience flow when doing psychotherapy. I can become so absorbed in my conversation with my patients that I lose track of time and feel a deep connection with them. Another "flow" experience is when I interact with workshop participants about some cogent issue of character or personality that I believe can be life transforming. In these moments, I frequently become so absorbed that I wish the encounter would never end.

Now is an opportunity for you to reflect on your own life experiences. Identify three times when you too were in the "flow." Describe them: What were you doing? What were you feeling? Most importantly, what was it about those experiences that created this feeling of "flow?"

1.

2.

3.

2. What Is Unique about Me?

Earlier I shared the story about my professional frustrations and the solution I experienced through my work with my personal coach, Margaret. I now urge you to discover your own uniqueness. As did I, identify six people who know you well. Contact them, and get their ideas about what they think is unique about you. Write what they say below:

Person 1

_____

_____

_____

Person 2

_____

_____

_____

Person 3

_____

_____

_____

Person 4

_____

_____

_____

Person 5

_____

_____

_____

Person 6

_____

_____

_____

3. About What Am I Enthusiastic?

Many people waste their time trying to fire themselves up. They invent all kinds of strategies to excite themselves into action. While this may briefly work, enthusiasm cannot be sustained over time through such gimmickry.

The task before you now is to uncover what it is that naturally excites your enthusiasm. For example, I find exciting helping my clinical patients and my business consultees evolve into all they can be. I get excited about helping my sons develop strength of character. And I find it exciting to help and support my wife in her own pursuit of happiness in life.

As you address this question, be careful to note that you may not be enthusiastic about some particular activity itself but, instead, the reason for doing it. I distinctly remember a housewife telling me she enthusiastically went about the onerous chore of cleaning her bathrooms. Seeing the incredulous look on my face, she explained that she viewed this chore as an expression of taking loving care of her family.

Now reflect on your enthusiasms. What lights your fire? What turns you on? What do you deeply care about? The answers to these questions, along with what about them excites you, can help you create your life's Passionate Purpose.

What Am I Doing When Excited	Why It Excites Me

4. What could I Do in Lift That Would Provide the Most Value, Make the Biggest Contribution, and Have the Most Positive Impact?

In helping people proactively take charge of their lives, Stephen Covey (1989) poses two profound questions:

1. "What is one thing that, if you did it consistently and excellently, would make a profoundly positive difference in your personal life?"
2. "What is one thing that, if you did it consistently and excellently, would make a profoundly positive difference in your professional life?"

My experience is that it takes people little time to answer these questions. But, the next and perhaps more important question is, "If you know that doing these would make such a difference, why aren't you doing them?"

Both the "what" and the "why not" questions are empowering. The "what" questions alert you to what exactly you need to do to produce both great results and great fulfillment. The "why not" question helps you figure out what blocks you from doing what's necessary to bring about your satisfaction and happiness.

Knowing the answers to these questions can also help you create your Passionate Purpose. Now please reflect on this question: What could you do that would have the greatest value, make the most positive impact, and make the biggest contribution in both your personal and professional life? To add meat to this question, make sure you note who would benefit and how: You? Your loved ones? Your friends and colleagues? Your clientele? Society at large?

In my personal life:

_____

_____

_____

_____

_____

In my professional life:

_____

_____

_____

_____

_____

5. What Kind of Person Would I like To Be?

To help you with this question, think of two people who you most admire and have made a big impact on your life. What qualities do they possess? When I asked myself this question, I actually identified six people: My mother and father; my English Literature teacher in college, Dr. Paul Grabel; my college basketball coach, Arad McCutchan; my psychology mentor, Dr. Albert Ellis; and my cousin, Bill Stocker. Each of these cherished individuals possessed qualities that have helped mold into me the positive qualities that give me satisfaction and pride.

I am sure you can easily identify at least two significant people of your own. Add more if you like. Do so now, along with their notable qualities. This too can contribute to creating your purpose.

	The Persons	Their Notable Qualities
1.	_____	_____
	_____	_____
2.	_____	_____
	_____	_____

Prompt Two: Create Your Purpose. Now that you are armed with all this introspective information, your second step is to create your life's Passionate Purpose. One of the mistakes people often make is to rush this. Don't. Take your time. Reflect on your answers to the five questions I posed above. You might want to carry them with you for a week or so and make additions or corrections before crafting your purpose. You might also want to make notes about themes or phrases you want to include.

Your Purpose can be written in any format that communicates to you. It can be a single phrase, a complete sentence, a poem, a brief paragraph, or even a song or a picture. The point is, your Purpose must speak to you without concern for what others may think. It is meant to reflect your passion and spark your drive and fulfillment.

By way of example, I first offer the purpose of Mike Krzyzewski, the Duke University basketball coach, holder of three NCAA championship trophies, two Olympic gold medals, and more wins than anyone in men's NCAA history. He stated: "I am not a basketball coach. I am a leader who coaches basketball. I have three goals with all my players – to make them a good student, a good citizen, and a good person" (Krzyzewskie, 2006).

Another example comes from Mahatma Gandhi, the man who liberated India from the rule of Great Britain by acting according to his Passionate Purpose:

Let the first act of every morning be to make the following resolve for the day:

I shall not fear anyone on earth.
I shall only fear God.
I shall not bear ill toward anyone.
I shall not submit to injustice from anyone.
I shall conquer untruth by truth.
And, in resisting untruth, I shall put up
with all suffering.

(Attenborough, 1982)

Lastly, I share with you my own Purpose in its complete form: "To make my life, the lives of my loved ones, and the lives of those with whom I relate and work perfect, as they want it. To do this, I will be consistently excellent in living, modeling, and teaching the strategies for effective and joyful living."

Now it's time to create a first draft your own Passionate Purpose. Remember to review your answers to the questions I posed. Once you have penned a first draft, carry it with you. Reflect on it. Make notes about changes you might want. After a week or two, compose your final version.

My Purpose

(First Draft)

_____

_____

_____

_____

_____

_____

_____

_____

_____

_____

My Purpose

(Final Draft)

_____

_____

_____

_____

_____

_____

_____

_____

_____

_____

_____

Prompt Three: Live Your Purpose. Now you have a start to your life's purpose in hand. While it hopefully inspires you, it is most likely too general to be of much practical use. To take it to the level of useful action, you need to plan exactly how you will manifest it throughout the fabric of your life.

Stephen Covey (1989) wisely suggests that the major roles we play in life can serve as vehicles through which to live out our purpose. I, for example, try to express mine through the following five roles, as an:

- Individual with a relationship with myself;
- Husband and father;
- Extended family member and friend;
- Clinical psychologist and organizational consultant;
- Teacher.

The question I ask myself is, "How can I help the people in each of these roles make their lives perfect, as they want them to be?" In answering this question, I was surprised at the numbers of opportunities I easily identified to act on my purpose. I might add that writing this book is one important way I discovered to live my purpose through my work.

So the next step in your workshop is to articulate some ways you might express your purpose through each major role you play in your life. You can borrow my categories or make a list your own. By connecting what you do to your purpose to each of your life roles, you will find it almost impossible to not experience passion, satisfaction, and happiness.

	My Roles	How Can I Express My Purpose?
1.	_____	_____
	_____	_____
	_____	_____
2.	_____	_____
	_____	_____
	_____	_____
3.	_____	_____
	_____	_____
	_____	_____
4.	_____	_____
	_____	_____
	_____	_____
5.	_____	_____
	_____	_____
	_____	_____

Additional Passionate Purpose Strategies

Congratulations. With the first draft of your Passionate Purpose in hand, you are now poised to bring more happiness into your life. But merely creating it is not sufficient. You must act on it – daily. Here then are five cognitive and five behavioral strategies to help you integrate your passionate purpose into your life so you can enjoy the rewards it can bring.

Cognitive Strategies

1. Take Responsibility

One of the more important decisions you will ever make is whether to live by the philosophy of Conditional Personal Responsibility (CPR) or Unconditional Personal Responsibility (UPR). Those who adopt Conditional Personal Responsibility (CPR) think that their ability to be happy is limited by their circumstances. They contend that, if only they had more education, money, or intelligence, for example, then they'd be happy. Holding that they are hopelessly limited by their circumstances, they believe they have no choice but to resignedly accept their lot and passively endure frustration, depression, and bitterness.

To the contrary, those who adopt the philosophy of Unconditional Personal Responsibility (UPR) see that their happiness is up to them, no matter what their circumstances may be. They live by the conviction that, while their circumstances may be difficult, it's their responsibility to figure out how to get around, through, or over them in order to create a happy life.

I hope you find your Passionate Purpose stimulating and exciting. However, you will only create happiness by acting on it. And, the degree to which you do will be determined by the choice you make between CPR or UPR. If you choose CPR, then you'll surely hesitate when circumstances go against you, if not give up and quit. But, if you choose UPR, then you'll likely persist to live your purpose despite the difficulties you encounter along the way. You thereby give yourself the best chance of creating the happy life you want.

2. Live It One Day at a Time

The adage "One Day at a Time" is a cornerstone of all twelve-step recovery programs. It serves to focus the person on abstinence for just today, not for the whole of his or her entire lifetime. This makes sobriety less daunting and more manageable.

On a larger level, the perspective of "One Day at a Time" can also guide you to live your whole life one day at a time. After all, all you have is today. The past no longer exists, and the future is yet to be. All that is real and available is now.

So now, for just today, focus on living your Passionate Purpose. Forget about yesterday. Ignore tomorrow. Start your day by asking: What are the opportunities I have to express my purpose today? When, where, and with whom can I do that? How can I act to do that? This focus will serve to connect your Passionate Purpose to your life as it unfolds today. In the process, every moment of today can be meaningful. So, immediately, today, focus on acting out your Passionate

Purpose in the here and now. Then, once you wake up tomorrow, do this again, and then again the next day, and on and on.

3. Adopt a Philosophy of Death

Remember the joke I told in this book's "Introduction" about the man who tripped and fell from a fifty-story building. As he fell past the twenty-seventh floor, someone inside shouted, "How's it going?" The falling man smiled and yelled back, "So far, so good."

This joke serves to remind us that the pavement awaits all of us. No one escapes death. It is the final destination for all of us. We're alive today, but one day we won't be. The truth is that we just don't know when that day will be. In fact, it could even be tomorrow.

As daunting as our inevitable death may be, facing this fact can be very valuable. It can remind us that today is the only day we know for sure that we will ever have. It can remind us that we had better not put off pursuing our happiness until tomorrow. It can remind us to fully live our Passionate Purpose today.

4. Savor Your Pleasure

Assuming that your Passionate Purpose reflects what you truly value, simply acting on it can provide you with a great deal of pleasure. For example, I take tremendous pleasure in working to make my patients' lives perfect as they want them to be, as I do in the writing of this book to hopefully help you make your life perfect as you want to be. Be sure to tune into this pleasure, as it is rewarding in and of itself, as well as motivating for you to keep up your efforts going forward in life.

5. Take Pride in What You Accomplish

Your Passionate Purpose is all about producing results. But they are not about just any results. They are about results that are truly meaningful to you. You therefore deserve to take pride in both your efforts to produce them, as well as in what you produce. Enjoy all of this. Be proud of it.

Behavioral Strategies

1. Keep It Front and Center

If your life is like mine, it's crammed full of all sorts of activities, chores, and responsibilities. I suspect that, like me, you also find it tempting to mindlessly hop from one task to another, doing your best to knock them out as fast as you can. In the process, you can easily lose sight of your Passionate Purpose. This hardly fits into the Passionate Purpose formula for happiness.

One of the things you can do to avoid this trap is to keep your Passionate Purpose front and center. Here are a few suggestions to help you do that. One is to set aside a few minutes at a regular time to review your upcoming week and make note of situations in which you can passionately express your purpose. I spend about a half hour each Sunday evening doing just that. You can also begin each day with a review of that day's upcoming activities, reminding yourself to express your Passionate Purpose through them. A third is to take a few minutes before special events. (e.g., a family dinner, an important business meeting, visiting in-laws) to connect them to your Purpose. Taking time to do these will keep you connected to your Passionate Purpose and afford you ample opportunities to feel rewarded and happy.

2. First Things First

Johan Wolfgang von Goethe wisely tells us, "Things that matter most must never be at the mercy of things which matter least." But how many times do we truly follow that advice? Far too often we cram our lives full of whatever is the next thing on the horizon, our latest whim, or the pressure to do what others want us to do. Sadly, what we find most important often takes a backseat. Worse yet, we let it fall by the wayside.

This is where your Passionate Purpose becomes invaluable. With it clear in your mind, you can make sure that what matters most never takes a second place to what matters least. All you have to do is follow the five-step process Stephen Covey outlined in his seminal book, *The Seven Habits Of Highly Effective People* (1989): (1) know what are the key roles you play in life; (2) note two or three important results you want to produce in each role that reflect your Passionate Purpose; (3) schedule an action to produce each result at a specific time on a specific day; (4) then, and only then, fill in the rest of your schedule with the other things that are of lesser importance, never letting them intrude on or supersede what is most important; and (5) act with commitment and integrity to honor your schedule.

3. Do What Makes a Difference

The truth is that we simply do not have time to do everything we want. Furthermore, even if we had unlimited time, many of the things that interest us are outside of our control. For example, most of us take seriously both our primary relationship and the issue of nuclear proliferation. While both of these concerns are on our radar, we have infinitely more influence over making the relationship with our significant other loving and lasting than preventing the spread of nuclear weapons.

In deciding how to live and express one's Passionate Purpose, it only makes sense to choose to do the things about which we can make a difference. With my Passionate Purpose being to help people make their lives perfect, as they want them to be, I ask myself: What can I do this week to help my wife prosper? What about my kids? How about my patients? With these people, I can act to make a difference, not with regard to the arms race.

4. Leverage Pleasure and Pain

It is a simple fact of human nature that we seek pleasure and avoid pain. That is why we find it so difficult to pass up that bowl of chocolate ice cream, but then find it so easy to avoid mowing the lawn, balancing the checkbook, or getting on the treadmill first thing in the morning. As these examples illustrate, pleasure and pain often run us to our detriment rather than to our benefit.

To help you follow through on your Passionate Purpose, you can intentionally use pleasure and pain to help motivate you to act. Specifically, you can reward yourself each time you act on it. One of my patients keeps a plastic cookie jar and a large bowl of marbles beside her bed. She puts a marble in the jar before bedtime for everything she did that day that expressed her Passionate Purpose. Then, when she has filled the jar, she treats herself to a special night on the town with her husband.

You too can similarly reward yourself, thereby providing yourself extra incentive. Each week decide what Passionate Purpose behavior you will reward. Then select a reward, preferably something that you find pleasurable that is available to you every day – that dessert after supper, the daily newspaper, your favorite music. Finally, reward yourself with that treat, but only if you have acted on your Passionate Purpose.

5. Enroll Support

I personally find the challenge of life so much easier when supported by others. I rely on my mentor to give me constructive feedback and encouragement about my writing. I turn to a trusted colleague for advice on treating my thornier patients. And I am grateful to have my loving wife who not only partners with me in meeting our joint responsibilities, but also supports me to the fullest in living my Passionate Purpose.

Support from others can be of tremendous help to you too in living your Passionate Purpose. Who could your go-to person be? What will you ask this person to do to support you? How often would it be best to meet? This person can not only serve to hold you accountable, but act as a combination coach and cheerleader.

Your Passionate Purpose Happiness Action Plan

Here now is the most important part of this chapter. It is your opportunity to brainstorm strategies you might want to include in your personalized, workable Happiness Action Plan (HAP). It need not be perfect, for you'll have a chance to revise it once you get to Chapter 9: "Creating Your Happiness Action Plan." But, get started as you don't have to wait until you've got the complete final package assembled. You can start the process of bringing more happiness into your life right now.

So, to begin, take a few minutes to review the contents of this chapter. Once you've done that, record below the latest draft of your Passionate Purpose. It states the burning "why" of your life – the reason for what you do on an hour-by-hour basis. Then list what you will do to express it through the significant roles in your life – where, when, and with whom. Next, note what additional cognitive and/or behavioral strategies you will apply to help you execute your purpose every day. Finally, follow through with action – right away, and then every day going forward. Please understand that none of the ideas or tools I've presented will make a difference unless you fully apply them. But, if you do, I promise you that you will reap the happiness benefits.

My Passionate Purpose: _____

_____

_____

_____

_____

_____

_____

My Roles	My Actions Where, When, With Whom
1. _____	_____
_____	_____
_____	_____
2. _____	_____
_____	_____
_____	_____
3. _____	_____
_____	_____
_____	_____
4. _____	_____
_____	_____
_____	_____
5. _____	_____
_____	_____
_____	_____

Additional Strategies I Will Use

Cognitive	Behavioral
1. _____	1. _____
_____	_____
_____	_____
2. _____	2. _____
_____	_____
_____	_____

3. _____   3. _____

_____   _____

_____   _____

4. _____   4. _____

_____   _____

_____   _____

5. _____   5. _____

_____   _____

_____   _____

Going Forward

The theme of this chapter is that acting according to your Passionate Purpose is a critical ingredient to creating a happy life. When you bring passion and purpose to what you do, you find meaning in your life and thereby experience satisfaction and fulfillment.

I urge you to begin to act on your Passionate Purpose – starting today and continuing one day at a time. See if you don't soon reap the happiness benefits. In the next chapter, I will lead you through the process of finding happiness with yourself. See you there.

Note

1 This workshop is adapted from chapter 3, "The Power of Passionate Purpose," of my book, *Developing Unrelenting Drive, Dedication, and Determination: A Cognitive Behavior Workbook*, published by Routledge in 2017, and from chapter 2, "The Power of Passionate Purpose: The Fuel That Stimulates Sustained High Energy, Enthusiasm, and Satisfaction," of my book, *On Becoming a Cognitive Behavioral Psychotherapist*, published by Routledge in 2018.

Notes

5

HAPPINESS WITH YOURSELF

Last Christmas, my brother gifted my family with a large crate of Florida oranges. The sweet smell of citrus filled the room before I even opened the lid. "Yum," I thought, my mouth watering.

Once I pried off the crate's top, I plunged my hand wrist-deep into the fruit. To my chagrin, what I pulled out was not a ripe, succulent orange, but one pockmarked, brown, and squishy. "Yuck," I said, then impulsively picked up the crate, oranges and all, carried it outside, and stuffed it into the garbage can.

What would you have done? Would you, like me, throw out the whole crate? Or would you toss only the one rotten orange and save all the rest for future pleasure? I suspect you'd choose the latter. To do otherwise would be foolish. After all, "One rotten orange doesn't spoil the whole bunch."

Well, I lied. I did what I suspect you would do. I tossed the one spoiled orange out and stored the rest in my basement refrigerator.

But, while most people would make the same choice we did with the oranges, they often do the opposite with regard to themselves. Following a stupid mistake, an embarrassing setback, or even some personal failing, they all too often trash both what they did and their whole self as well.

This tendency to go from damning what we do to damning who we are probably accounts for more human unhappiness than anything else. For if we seriously denigrate ourselves, it follows that we will most likely impair ourselves in any number of ways. We will surely experience copious amounts of anxiety and insecurity, as well as guilt, depression, and shame. We will likely become either excessively driven for perfection or withdraw into passivity and avoidance. We will easily be needy and dependent, in the process sacrificing our own wants and desires in order to gain the favor from others. We will in all likelihood become overly sensitive to slights, thinking that what others say somehow diminishes us. We will find it hard to focus on our own goals and underachieve.

Indeed, many of the people I have treated over the years developed just these kinds of symptoms as a result of their self-damning. Take, for example, the despondent divorcee who concluded that, because she failed at her marriage, she was a failure. Then there was the young bulimic who thought she only had worth if her body was perfect. Consider the professional writer who avoided paper and pencil lest he fail at his craft and be seen as the second rate artist he secretly perceived himself to be. How about the businessman who obsessed over every decision for fear he'd make a mistake and incur eternal damnation. Then there was the promiscuous twenty-something who connected her self-worth to the attention of men. Lastly consider the young man who used both drugs and apathy to alleviate anxiety over being rejected by women.

These all too common stories beg us to ask perhaps the most important question of all, one posed by Albert Ellis back in 1972. Since people's estimation of their own self is so critical to their long-range happiness, how can we get them to view themselves so that, no matter the quality of their performance, and no matter how much or little they may be valued by others, they invariably accept and honor themselves?

The answer to this question will probably shock you. It is to convince people to never judge themselves, to never, ever hold themselves as all good or all bad, all worthwhile or all worthless. It is to convince people to live without "self-esteem" – to give it up, relinquish it, destroy it.

"What?" I can almost hear you scream. "I've spent a lifetime trying to feel good about myself, to love myself, to have high self-esteem. Now you tell me you want me to give all that up?"

That's exactly right. I do want you to give that up. Self-esteem is not your ally, but your enemy. If you want to consistently experience happiness with yourself, you've got to give up self-esteem.

And replace it with what?

The answer is the breakthrough strategy of Unconditional Self-Acceptance (USA). If you decide to adopt this USA view of your Self, you will virtually eliminate all depression and anxiety from your life, as well as almost always experiencing peace-of-mind. Moreover, by unconditionally accepting yourself, you open the door to benefiting from the additional self-happiness strategies I will share later in this chapter. So, please read on with an open mind, with hope and enthusiasm, and with the intention to make Unconditional Self-Acceptance work for you.

Breakthrough Strategy Two: Unconditional Self-Acceptance

The Cycle of Life

To understand exactly what Unconditional Self-Acceptance means, I start by sharing what the existential philosopher, Jean Paul Sartre (1943), called The

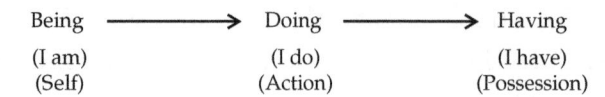

Figure 5.1 The Cycle of Life

Cycle of Life. As illustrated in Figure 5.1, he asserted that the life cycle starts with Being. That is, at the first moment of human life – whenever that may be, whether at conception, in utero, or at birth – there now exists a brand-spanking new Being, a new Self if you will. If able to speak, this infant would simply say, "I am." That would be it. There would be no descriptors or qualifiers, such as, "I am a baby," "I am a girl," or even "I am a human." She would just say, "I am," pure and simple, with no Self-Definition or Self-Judgment to follow.

From Being then comes Doing. The Being's early doings are quite primitive – sleeping, digesting, crying. But gradually, as the nervous system matures, and as experiences accumulate, the doings become more and more complex and sophisticated until, at some point, this Being can do such things as think abstractly, complete complex tasks, and communicate meaningfully with other Beings.

Completing the Cycle of Life, then, Doing leads to Having. Over time, this Being comes to have or possess all sorts of things, including personal Haves (e.g., height and weight, an IQ, a personality, skills, values and desires); role Haves (e.g., spouse, parent, sibling, friend); and object Haves (e.g., a job, money, a house, artwork, vehicles).

So that's Sartre's Cycle of Life. It's a one-way street, left to right, from Being to Doing to Having, not the other way around. What is important to take away from this are these two points:

(1) This Being existed as a Self, whole and intact, before he or she did any of his or her Doings and before he or she came to possess any Haves;
(2) While the doer of all these Doings and the possessor of all these Havings, this Being is not limited to or equal to any one of these.

Perverting the Cycle of Life

Perversion One: Self-Defining. According to Sartre (1943), we pervert The Cycle of Life when we define our Being – that is, who we are, our Self – by what we Do and/or what we Have (see Figure 5.2).

By the way of example, it would be incorrect of me to say that I am a psychologist. I indeed practice psychology on weekdays between 9:30 AM and 6:30 PM, but I also do many other things as well. For example, I eat breakfast, work out

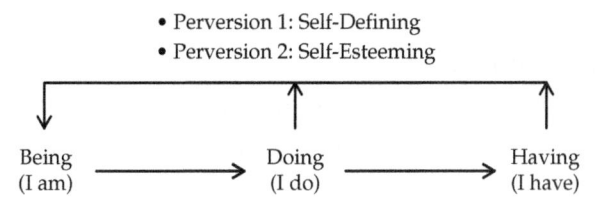

Figure 5.2 The Cycle of Life Perverted

on my treadmill, write books and papers, and do hundreds of other things. So, while practicing or doing psychology is something significant I do, I literally am not a psychologist. Precisely stated, "I am a Being that does psychology," among many other things.

Likewise, for me to tell you that "I am a father" would pervert the truth. Stated most accurately, "I am a Being – a Self – who has children and who does fathering, but I do many other things as well. None of these Do's and Have's define me, the Being." To belabor the point, it would be incorrect for me to even declare that "I am a man." This too is not so. I have the gender of male, but this one quality is only one among scores others I have.

"All right," you may say, "I understand conceptually what you're saying, but, outside the hallowed halls of academia, what's that got to do with me being happy with myself?"

Well, a lot, actually, and it's not good. For one, when you define your Being by what you do or have, you inevitably throw away your freedom of choice. If, for example, I define my Self as a psychologist, I will find it next to impossible to stop doing psychology. Why? Because, by no longer doing psychology, I not only lose the pleasures I derive from doing it, but I also lose who I am as well – my Being, my Self. I imprison myself into only doing this one thing, no matter how sour or toxic the experience may become, because, by ceasing to do it, I would lose myself as well.

Second, this Self-Defining perversion can also easily lead to a major depressive reaction. That's exactly what happens to the parent who suffers from what's called the empty nest syndrome. For example, when a woman defines herself as a mother, she not only misses her children when they leave home, but she can also easily fall prey to the despondency that comes from losing her sense of herself as well. By her own self-definition, she now is a nothing, and her life has become meaningless. The same can be true of the retiring executive, the ex-athlete, and any number of other categories of people who foolishly define themselves by what they do or have.

Perversion Two: Self-Esteeming. If the Self-Defining perversion is not enough, we humans also pervert The Cycle of Life when we Self-Esteem. Think about it. To Self-Esteem, we must first define our Self by some selected do or have, say practicing psychology, and then judge, rate, or esteem our whole Self by how well we do on this one activity or quality. So, once I define my Self as a psychologist, then it follows that I will almost inevitably conclude that I am a good person, a success, if I do psychology well, thus having high Self-Esteem. But, by such a self-definition, I will conclude that I am a total failure if I do psychology poorly, bringing on a sense of low Self-Esteem.

Notice that this is the same perspective you would have to hold to throw out all the oranges if you found one rotten one in the crate. Also, notice that all the unhappy people I described earlier in this chapter embodied both the Self-Definition and the Self-Esteeming perversions. If they had only represented their Being by the crate and all their Do's and Have's by the oranges, then they would never have thrown out their whole crate of oranges – their whole Selves – because of one rotten orange.

Unconditional Self-Acceptance Defined

If the perversions of Self-Defining and Self-Esteeming are barriers to experiencing happiness with yourself, then Unconditional Self-Acceptance (USA) is the royal road to personal happiness. To return to the orange analogy, think again of your Self (your Being) as the crate and all your actions (your Do's) and your qualities (your Have's) as the oranges. You, the crate, contains hundreds, if not thousands of oranges – discrete acts and traits accumulated over a lifetime. Many of your oranges are ripe and luscious – your good deeds, successes, and virtuous qualities. But, being human and fallible, some of your oranges are inevitably bruised, shriveled, even rotten – your mistakes and faults. When you run across a damaged orange, you may dislike it, regret it, even work to rid yourself of it, but you never – ever – denigrate, damn, or throw away your whole crate of oranges.

Imagine if the divorcee I mentioned before had thought, "I failed with him, but that one failure doesn't turn me into a total failure." Or if the bulimic had concluded, "I want to look fit and sexy, but my body is just one part of me and hardly rates the whole of me as a totally good or bad person." Or, how about if the writer had taken the stance, "The worst thing that will happen is that I'll create something less than sterling, but that mediocre performance is just something I did, not who I am." Freed of Self-Defining and Self-Esteeming, wouldn't these people's lives be so much more peaceful and happy?

So that's the essence of Unconditional Self-Acceptance. You separate yourself from your actions and qualities. You accept that, as a fallible, imperfect human, you will often perform well, but you will also at times err. When you do perform well, you take pride in what you do, but you don't deify your whole Self. When you act badly, you may regret or even criticize your behavior, but you refuse to flog your whole Self as bad. You always unconditionally accept your Self as just Being, without any self-definition or self-judgment whatsoever.

The bottom line is that, when you practice Unconditional Self-Acceptance, you solidify the ground of happiness under your feet. You...

- Inspire within yourself a sense of peace since you can err without becoming an error, fail without becoming a failure, and act badly without becoming a bad person;
- Prompt the boldness that can lead to success, pleasure, and fun, without suffering nagging fear and anxiety;
- Give birth to a deep sense of well-being and happiness.

From Theory to Practice

At this point, I want to tell you that there is both good and bad news. The bad news is that you have most likely lived by these two perversions your whole life. How do I know this? I know so because our whole society inundates us with them. Look at the world of sports, our educational system, the entertainment complex, our financial institutions, the way advertising works, and on and on. As a culture, we roundly deify those who succeed and devilify those who don't. It is the rare individual who has resisted being brainwashed into both Self-Defining and Self-Esteeming.

But don't fret. There is also good news: With effort and fortitude, you can reprogram the way you think about yourself. You can learn to unconditionally accept yourself without self-defining or judging. Untold numbers of others have done it, and so can you. Start right now with what follows.

1. Remember that how you think is your choice. You can choose to think along the lines of these two happiness-destroying perversions or you can choose to adopt Unconditional Self-Acceptance. I vote for Unconditional Self-Acceptance. How about you? Make your commitment right now. Choose between the two following statements below.

I, _____, fully commit to living by the twin perversions of Self-Defining and Self-Esteeming. I will damn my whole self whenever I err, fail, or find a fault in myself.

Signature _____

Date: _____

I, _____, will refuse to define myself by any of my action, qualities, or possessions. Furthermore, I will never judge, rate, or esteem my whole self as good or bad, worthwhile or worthless, a success or a failure. Instead, I will fully accept myself as alive and human, without definition or judgment, and go about this business of finding happiness with total, unconditional self-acceptance.

Signature _____

Date: _____

2. If you've chosen to endorse Unconditional Self-Acceptance, then here are three strategies to help you habituate it into the way you think.

   (1) Identify two situations in which you tend to judge your whole Self. Note what you could tell yourself in these two situations to help you unconditionally accept yourself, despite any mistakes you may make or flaws you may possess? Practice them.

   1.

   _____

   _____

   2.

   _____

   _____

   (2) Make a commitment to spend two minutes, six times a day (breakfast, mid-morning, lunch, mid-afternoon, supper, and bedtime), drawing the distinction between your Being or Self and your Doings and

Havings. Remind yourself to neither define nor judge yourself as either all good or all bad as you progress through the day.

(3) Practice applying Unconditional Self-Acceptance to others. That is, practice only rating other peoples' behaviors and traits as good or bad, but never them as a whole person. This is Unconditional Other Acceptance.

Additional Self-Happiness Strategies

I urge you to put the philosophy of Unconditional Self-Acceptance into practice. It will do wonders for your emotional well-being. To further help you find happiness with yourself, I now provide six additional strategies you may find productive. As you study them, think about which ones you think might be helpful to include in the Happiness Action Plan you will complete in Chapter 9.

Cognitive Strategies

1. Focus on Your Positives

There is a profound psychological truth: What you focus on determines your mood. Out of the panoply of events in your life, you will enrich your mood if you focus on the positives. To the contrary, by focusing on the negatives, you will bring yourself down. This principle holds true with regard to yourself as well. If you fall into the trap of focusing mostly on your mistakes and faults, you'll block out your chance for happiness.

This proved to be the case with Elizabeth. Growing up, she received so much criticism from her mother that she learned to mostly pay attention to her shortcomings. Her negative self-focus kept her mood in the gutter and forced her to only hope for happiness.

Elizabeth resisted change at first. Having spent her whole life focused on her negatives, she found it automatic to do so. But I gradually wore her down until she started noticing her good qualities. As this focus grew, so did her growing sense of contentment and happiness.

Here then are five strategies that can help you focus on your positives. The more frequently and fervently you practice them, the sooner you will habituate this focus.

1. Make a list of your positive qualities. Don't be shy. Remember what Mohammed Ali said: "It ain't bragging if you can do it." Consult with others to help you compile this list. Then schedule four five-minute meetings

with yourself each day – breakfast, lunch, supper, bedtime – to review your positives.

2. Keep a notebook next to your bed. Before tucking yourself in at night, list three positive things you did that day. These may be small or large – it makes no difference. Be sure to pat yourself on the back for these positive actions.

3. Brag on yourself. Practice telling someone you trust something you did that was positive or appropriate. The more you do this, the more natural it will become.

4. Hang out with the people who care about and affirm you. They know you have faults, but care about you anyway. Their affirmations can be a reminder that you are indeed endowed with good qualities.

5. To help you focus on your own positives, make it a point to also give three others a compliment each day. Remember: What goes around, comes around.

2. Be Perfectly Imperfect

Forty-two-year-old Mary is a family physician who practices at a state-supported teaching hospital. She is blessed with the opportunity to impact the lives of untold numbers of people, both the patients she treats and those her students will treat for years to come.

Yet she suffered from happiness-crippling anxiety that destroyed her peace of mind. She spent her Sundays dreading going to work the next day. She walked from one patient to another with a knot in her stomach. Her only relief came when she buried herself in her administrative duties. But this only partially distracted her from the next clinic that loomed in the back of her mind.

When Mary walked into my office, I noticed by her furrowed brow and pursed lips that she enjoyed little happiness. After she told me the details of her symptoms, we had the following exchange.

DR. G: Think for minute, Mary. You're home alone on Sunday with anxiety gnawing at you. What goes through your mind the second before you begin to feel that way?

MARY: I've got clinic tomorrow.

DR. G: I know, but what do you tell yourself that is so horrible about that?

MARY: I might make a mistake and embarrass myself in front of my students.

Dr. G: Ah, but, so what if you did? Why would that be so horrible?

MARY: I'm a physician. I can't afford a mistake.

Dr. G: But, Mary, how in the world can you pull that off? How can you go through your professional life, much less a single day, and never make a mistake? Sounds impossible to me. Even doctors are imperfect and fallible, aren't they?

MARY: Of course. But we're taught in medical school that, God forbid, we should ever make a mistake!

Dr. G: Well, that's a shame, because that sets up the anxiety you suffer from. Think about it. You've taken an admirable desire to do your best with each of your patients. And then you've convinced yourself that you absolutely must or need to be perfect. With that "must be perfect" expectation banging around in your head, you bring on this misery every time you go to battle. Do you see?

MARY: I do.

Dr. G: And what does this demand for perfection get you?

MARY: My anxiety.

Dr. G: Yes, and little, if any, happiness and pleasure in your work.

MARY: Sad, but true.

I'm happy to report that Mary worked hard in her therapy. Over several months of intensive attitude adjustment, she gradually let go of the perfectionism that blocked her ability to experience life as a happy person. She learned to accept herself, even with her imperfections. As she did, her anxiety dissipated and her ability to enjoy her work increased many-fold.

Mary can be a role model for you. Like her, you can accept that you are a fallible human being who will, by your human nature, make countless errors in life. None of these define who you are or rate you as a failure. Get real. Instead of demanding that you be perfect, demand that you be imperfect.

Below are five practices that can help you loosen the grip perfectionism has on you. The degree to which you use them will be the degree to which you claim your self-happiness birthright. But remember that breaking any habit and building a new one takes time and effort.

(1) Identify three situations in which you fall into the trap of thinking you have to do perfectly. For each, write an antiperfection message you will recite to yourself so as to deal with the situation.

(2) Use your mistakes as opportunities to learn and grow. When you make a mistake, say to yourself "Good, I goofed; now I can learn something valuable for the future."

(3) When you do make a mistake, remind yourself this is perfect opportunity to practice Unconditional Self-Acceptance. Forcefully remind yourself that your mistake was merely an orange, not your whole crate.

(4) Purposely make one mistake a day. Wear a tie that doesn't match your shirt. Praise President Trump at a Democratic gathering, or announce your admiration for Nancy Pelosi at a Republican rally. Loudly request mustard for your scrambled eggs at a brunch with friends. Observe that no cataclysmic consequences befall you when you act foolishly.

(5) Notice when others make mistakes. Remind yourself that you are not a special case and that fallibility is not exclusive to you. Also note that their mistake is also just one of their oranges and doesn't reflect on their whole crate or themselves.

3. Want, Don't Need

By mid-December, my then fourteen-year-old son Gabriel entered full Christmas mode. His list for Santa started big and grew bigger by the day. It included a surround-sound speaker system, various gizmos for his computer, and a new iPhone. My wife and I looked at each other in horror. "His appetite could easily gobble our savings," she said.

The truth of the matter, though, was that Gabriel was neither gluttonous nor narcissistic. He simply shared a characteristic all humans possess. With his human mind, he found it easy to think he needed what he wanted; that is, he concluded that, because he wanted something, he absolutely must have that thing he wanted. "I want that toy" quickly transformed into "I need that toy" in the blink of an eye.

See if that's not true for you. Pick any day of your choosing and observe how many times you think in terms of need. "I've *got to* get there on time." "I *have to* do well on that project." "I *must* impress them."

The sad fact is that this mental gymnastic – convincing yourself you need what you want – accounts for a huge amount of misery. Back to Gabriel. By holding his wants as a necessity, Gabriel made himself anxious for fear he wouldn't get what he wanted. But that was only on the front end. If his mom and I would fail to deliver to him the iPhone, he would have been devastated for, in his mind, he would be deprived of something he deemed necessary.

But here's a news flash. Despite what you've been taught, you have no needs, except for food, water, shelter, and air. Think about it. No one has yet died from not getting what they want, whether that be something tangible, like an iPhone, or something intangible such as love, affection, and approval from some valued others. Sure, they often experience disappointment, sadness, and sometimes even deep grief, but they only bring devastation on themselves when they believe they must have what they want.

Here are the takeaways. One, be a big wanter. Two, once you figure out what you want, work your heart out to make it a reality. After all, seeking and savoring pleasure and happiness is what gives life gusto. But, no matter what it is that you want, never convince yourself that you need it. By doing that, you'll experience gratification when you get your want fulfilled, but you will never be destroyed when you don't.

What follows are five strategies to help you learn to want without needing.

1. To rid yourself of the notion that you need what you want, first understand that such thinking makes no sense. Here are five reasons why you never need what you want.

    (1) The concept of need falsely implies necessity. But, if you really think about it, necessity means that it is a matter of life and death to get what you want. Isn't that silly? We only need, really need, what sustains our life – food, air, shelter, and water. Everything else is only desirable, adding to the quality of life.

    (2) Need implies that getting what you want is the only thing that really matters in life. If you don't get that outcome, you have nothing else in life to enjoy. Again, that's nonsense. Just because you fail to get one thing you want hardly erases all the other pleasures and prizes that exist in your life.

    (3) Thinking you need what you want is illogical. It may be true that you want something, even deeply and profoundly, but it doesn't logically follow that because you want it, you need it.

    (4) When you're thinking you need what you want, you are unwittingly being narcissistic. Simply said, you don't run the universe. It is pretty grandiose for you to say that what you want – to succeed, to be loved, to be treated well, to have things work out – must be granted.

    (5) Holding your wants as needs is not in your best interest. To think you need anything makes you feel desperate, anxious, insecure, for where is the guarantee you'll fulfill your needs. Furthermore, you'll feel miserable when things go wrong and just relieved when things go right.

To help you be happy, think through the above and understand that you have no needs, except for those that sustain life. Then apply this logic to everything you face as you go about your daily life.

2. Inventory your life and pinpoint what you absolutely believe you need or must have. Might it be the approval of others, and, if so, would it be with virtually everybody or only with a select few? Do you think you have to have some tangible object that you desire (e.g., that new car), some pleasurable outcome (e.g., the high from pornography), or the avoidance of some onerous experience (e.g., the boredom and frustration of balancing your checkbook)? Perhaps you think you need to perform well in some arena – socially occupationally, creatively – or else you'll just die? Tackle these so-called needs one at a time. Take whatever time is necessary to go over why it's not true that you absolutely need this outcome, using the arguments above. Once you have conquered one "need," do the same with the next one until you've surrendered all of them.

3. Make a habit of not using any need words or phrases; in addition to the words, "I need," they include "I've got to," "I have to," "I must," and "I should." Instead, use words such as "want," "like to," "desire," "hope for," "prefer," and "it would be better if." Say what you mean and mean what you say.

4. Practice self-denial. That is, look for opportunities to delay gratifying yourself with something desired or, if you want to go full throttle, deny yourself that gratification entirely. For example, put off that bowl of ice cream for an hour or pass it up entirely. While doing so, be sure to remind yourself that, as much as you might want it, you won't die without it.

5. Always enjoy the pleasures that come from having your wants satisfied. After all, these pleasures can add up to much happiness in life. While doing so, be careful to not let yourself fall into the trap of thinking you must continue to have this pleasure. As a bonus, actively practice indoctrinating yourself with the idea that, while you greatly like the pleasure, it is indeed not necessary.

Behavioral Strategies

1. Do What Gives You Pleasure – Every Day

Fifty-two-year-old Sean presented quite a sight when I met him. He wore his salt-and-pepper hair pulled back into a ponytail that hung halfway down his back. He wore a red flannel shirt tucked into faded jeans held tight by a belt with a silver buckle the size of a dollar bill. On his feet were calf-high work boots laced tight over the bottoms of his pants legs, the better to keep ticks away, he explained. I couldn't help but wonder what Grizzly Adams was doing in my office.

Sean described the depression that weighed him down most every day. I probed until I uncovered the culprits that blocked any chance for him to experience the happiness he so much craved. Not surprisingly, he expected himself to be perfect, damned himself when he wasn't, and mostly focused on his negative qualities while ignoring his good deeds. He could have been the poster child for Unhappiness with Myself Unlimited.

Sean took to therapy like a bear to honey. He embraced my input, followed through on his between-session assignments, and worked hard to unconditionally accept himself. He learned to damn his mistakes but never himself. He sloughed off his expectation for perfection. And he acknowledged that he indeed possessed tons of positive qualities.

As you can imagine, the more Sean changed his negative thoughts about himself, the more his depression drained away. One day, he ambled into my office and said, "Doc, I think I'm over my depression."

"Great," I said. "You sure worked hard at it."

"Thanks," he said. "Now I think I want to get some of that happiness."

And that's what we did. I explained to him that once he resolved to be happy, his task became simple. It was to discard those things that lead to suffering and engage in what brought him happiness.

With that, I instructed him to take a week to think of four or five things that, if he made these a regular part of his life, would bring him more happiness. Here's what he brought in the next week:

1. Doing my artwork;
2. Having an intimate relationship with a soulmate;
3. Communing with like-minded friends and colleagues;
4. Getting back to nature.

After presenting this to me, Sean said, "No wonder I don't have happiness. I have none of these in my life."

"So let's get to work creating them," I replied.

Sean started small. He chose to do his artwork an hour each day and to regularly get outside to walk in the woods. He also made a point to meet up weekly with a friend and enrolled in an online dating site. He's still going through the process, but I can report that his happiness grows steadily as he continues to build pleasure into each day.

If Sean can create such happiness results, so can you. To immediately begin to do so, you would be wise to pursue the following:

(1) Make a list of as many small things as you can that would bring you pleasure. Don't censure yourself; nothing is too small or silly, so long as it contributes to you having a good day. Then, most importantly, make sure you build in at least one of these pleasures each day, starting today.

(2) Make a list of bigger things you'd like to do that would bring you pleasure, but which may not be available on a daily basis. Examples might be attending a concert, spending a weekend at the beach, or having dinner with close friends. This gives you something to look forward to. Schedule one of these at least once a month.

(3) List the things you find negative in your life – things you find annoying, frustrating, dislikable. Focus on one each week and follow the wisdom of the Serenity Prayer – courageously work to rid those from your life you can while gracefully accepting those you can't.

(4) Identify the people you find toxic? Without damning them, either minimize your contact with them or eliminate them entirely from your life.

(5) Each night before bedtime, review the pleasures you had that day. Relive them, savor them, and be thankful for them.

2. Speak up for Yourself

How many times have you agreed to do something when you really wanted to say "no"? What about the times you've compliantly accepted a "no" from somebody when everything inside you screamed, "Speak up and go for what you want."

I know I have on more occasions than I'd like to admit. I bet you have too. We can all cite examples where we look back, slap ourselves on the forehead, and exclaim, "Why in the world didn't I…?"

For forty-two-year-old Jody, her passive compliance wasn't some occasional lapse of assertiveness. No, hers was a compulsive drive to sacrifice her own desires for the benefit of others.

Why would this intelligent, accomplished woman so habitually deny herself what she herself wanted? Why would she favor the well-being of others over her own? Why would she sacrifice her own pleasure to make others happy?

Listen to the conversation Jody and I had during her second psychotherapy session.

DR. G: So, Jody, your colleague at work asked you to help him complete his report over the weekend and you said "Yes," even though you had plans to go skiing. Right?

JODY: Right.

DR. G: What do you think motivated you to self-sacrifice like you did?

JODY: I just wanted to help out.

DR. G: Maybe. But that was a pretty major sacrifice you made. Let's go a little deeper. Finish this sentence for me: "I have to help him, even though I'll pay the price, because..."

JODY: His time is more valuable than mine.

DR. G: Now we're getting somewhere. Let me ask you this. In your mind, why is his time more valuable than yours?

JODY: That's the way I was raised. I was never good enough for my parents. I guess I just don't matter. Other people matter more than I do.

Clearly Jody operated from the belief that her whole self rated less than that of others. And look at the results for her in holding such a self-belief – the forfeit of time and energy, the denial of her own pleasure and fun, the taking on of the hassles and frustrations of others. In this case, Jody gave up a valued ski outing and instead labored over a tedious report all weekend. Multiply this by dozens of such examples per year and you'll see the opportunities for happiness she squandered.

It took Jody several months of intense therapeutic work to shift to more self-accepting thinking, plus lots of practice in acting assertively. But, as she did, she rid many unwanted, unnecessary, and onerous tasks from her life, carved out much more time for her own relaxation and enjoyment, and elevated pleasure and happiness to new levels.

Jody accomplished all this by speaking up for yourself, and so can you. Consider taking on the following:

(1) Identify the situations in which you normally self-sacrifice. They may be with your significant other, your children, your extended family, your friends, or your colleagues. Make a vow to refrain from immediately saying "yes" when these situations arise. Think of a response you can give (e.g., "Give me a little time to think about that and I'll get back to you.") to buy time to reflect on what you really want to do.

(2) Create a standard "no" response for situations in which "no" is appropriate. For example: "I'd like to help you out, but this is not a good time for me to do so. Sorry." Practice it at home in private until you have it well memorized. Then say it in real life.

(3) Determine to say "no" to someone once a day for the next month. Notice that, when you do, the heavens do not rain down boulders, lightning, or apocalyptic debris upon you. You'll find it will get easier and easier the more you practice.

(4) Identify situations in which you refrain from making requests of others, as if you have no right to do so. In the spirit of "I matter," force yourself to ask for what you want.

(5) When you do ask for a favor or assertively state your preference, pat yourself on the back. Remind yourself that you are rightfully the most important person to you in the world.

3. Lighten Up and Laugh

Life can be difficult, sometimes even tragic. I think of the mother whose teenage daughter was killed in a car accident, the number of youngsters who suffer some kind of brutal abuse, the young college student paralyzed from the waist down following a sports injury. My heart goes out to these poor souls.

Often, though, we react to relatively minor setbacks as if they amounted to calamities of the worst sort. We fail a math test, are criticized by our significant other, or say a foolish thing at a social gathering. All too often we take ourselves far too seriously. We hold onto our mistakes, the episodic disapprovals we get from others, and our occasional failures as deathly serious.

I have a sure-fire antidote for you. Lighten up and laugh, especially at your own foibles and peccadilloes.

Years ago, as an ex-basketball star, my high school invited me to speak at a pep rally before an important game. I wrote out my speech and rehearsed it many times in front of my bathroom mirror until I got it down pat. To whip the student body into a frenzy, I planned to carry in my pocket a handful of newspaper clippings predicting my team's demise, pull them out at the right moment, rip them to shreds, and throw them to the floor in disgust. I envisioned that everyone in the auditorium would blow the roof off.

I felt nervous walking onto the stage, but soldiered on and did pretty well until I reached the moment of truth. I slowly looked around the room and said to the entire student body, "The sportswriters say we have no chance, but we are the Bulldogs, and this is what I think of them." I grabbed the clippings and shot my hand in the air, ready for the grand finale. But, my hands trembled so much that the students could spot my nervousness.

The auditorium burst into a wave of laughter.

I stood stunned. But, miracle of miracles, the absurdity of the situation hit me smack in my head. A smile crossed my face, which morphed into a belly laugh.

Above the laughter, I shouted, "Hey guys, this is exactly how the Bears are going to feel when we take the court."

With that, I tore the clipping into shreds and threw them up into the air like confetti. All two thousand people in the auditorium – students and teachers alike – stood and cheered even louder and longer than I had hoped.

Talk about making lemonade out of lemons. At that moment, I discovered one of life's lessons: I don't have to take myself so seriously. Nobody – except me – expects me to be God's gift to speechmaking. When I lighten up about myself, I open the door to humor and laughter – and to pleasure.

Try these simple suggestions and see if you don't find yourself enjoying more happiness in your life:

1. Be willing to laugh at yourself. Finding your peccadilloes humorous can aide you in accepting yourself as a fallible human being, never perfect, without any negative self-judgment.

2. Laugh with, but never at, others. Remember that most people haven't read this book and, unfortunately, take themselves far too seriously. You may offend them and hurt their feelings.

3. Regularly expose yourself to humor. Read a funny book. Listen to a recording of George Carlin, Woody Allen, or Steve Martin. Watch a funny movie or TV show. Go to a comedy club. There are many opportunities to indulge yourself with the lighter side of life. Take advantage of them.

4. Enjoy a good joke. Welcome them when offered. Open yourself up to a good guffaw. The Internet is full of jokes, organized by topic and category, some tasteless and outrageous, others clever and delightful, all potential side-splitters. Find them, enjoy them, and have a good laugh. Better yet, share them with others.

5. Keep an eye out for life's absurdities. When you run across them, let yourself be amused. Notice how sports fans take their teams losing as dire as the specter of death. Observe the gentleman who fumes because his steak is not cooked exactly to his liking. How about the motorist who sits with his car idling through the entirety of the green light. Life's little circuses offer an endless supply of humor.

Your Happiness with Self Action Plan

So far in this chapter I have provided you with a paradigm of Self, Unconditional Self-Acceptance, that can not only free you from the miseries of anxiety and depression but can also bring you peace of mind. I have also shared six additional strategies that can add immensely to finding happiness with your Self. They too can bring you untold amounts of pleasure.

I hasten to add, however, that none of these strategies will be useful unless you act on them. Remember what I said in the Introduction: "If it's going to be, it's up to me." So, in the spirit of you being totally responsible for bringing happiness into your life, I urge you to continue to develop your Happiness Action Plan. To prepare yourself, I suggest you page through this chapter to refamiliarize yourself with its ideas and strategies. Then take your time to respond to the following two prompts. These can help you decide on what may work for you. Be focused, be positive, and have fun.

Prompt One: Becoming Unconditionally Self-Accepting. To help your endorse and habitualize Unconditional Self-Acceptance, select two strategies from those suggested on pages 81–91. For each, note exactly what you will do and where and when you will do it.

USA Strategy	What	Where/When
1. _____	_____	_____
_____	_____	_____
2. _____	_____	_____
_____	_____	_____

Prompt Two: Additional Self-Happiness Strategies. Select two additional self-happiness strategies that you think would increase your happiness quotient. Again, determine what you will do to use that strategy and where and when you will do it.

Strategy	What	Where/When
1. _____	_____	_____
_____	_____	_____
2. _____	_____	_____
_____	_____	_____

Great job. You've now added ideas that you can include in your Happiness Action Plan. But remember that your happiness is totally up to you – you don't have to wait for the finished product before you begin to use the strategies. Begin doing them now if you wish.

Going Forward

With the completion of this chapter, you have come a long way in bringing lasting happiness to your life. While hopefully holding a Passionate Purpose, you now have ideas as to how you can begin to work diligently to find enduring Happiness with Yourself. Take your time reflecting on this chapter, but, when ready, forge ahead into the next chapter, "Happiness with Others." I look forward to working with you when you get there.

Notes

6

HAPPINESS WITH OTHERS

It is the rare individual who doesn't find pleasure in bonding with others. To be sure, finding love and affection is a universal drive, one, when satisfied, not only provides pleasure but contributes to well-being and happiness as well. Accordingly, later in this chapter, I will describe a few proven, powerful strategies to help you generate happiness in your interpersonal life.

Before I get you there, I want to remind you of an inescapable fact of human life: We do not live among saints or angels, but with quite fallible human beings. Our lovers, friends, acquaintances, and even strangers will at times treat us poorly. Being fallible, they will bring their quirks, idiosyncrasies, and emotional problems to these interactions with us. They will regularly commit sins of commission, by saying and doing things we don't like, and sins of omission, by not doing things we do like.

Alas, that's the reality of living with other human beings. Even those who deeply love us will periodically act impatiently, irritably, even rudely. At other times, they will ignore us, forget to follow through on promises, and withhold affection. The question is not whether they will do this, but when.

During my thirty-five years of clinical practice, I have heard just about every type of interpersonal complaint. The wise individuals, the ones who rarely end up in my office, take these interpersonal missteps in stride. They realize that it is impossible for their fellow human beings to always act saintly. They gracefully chalk their misbehaviors up to the inevitable byproduct of human fallibility. They then either let the sin slide, going about their own business of being happy, or they calmly sit down and talk it out. Either way, they get on with life.

But many people, certainly those who seek my help, often don't react so wisely. They respond with deep hurt and anger, either lashing out with righteous indignation or carrying their grievances as prized possessions, nurturing them, holding them tight to their chest, sometimes for weeks and even months. By responding in this way, they create for themselves two problems for the price of one: They first experience the onerous behavior of the other person; second, they also suffer the happiness-contaminating feelings of anger and hurt.

Do you recognize yourself reacting this way? Jenny sure could. This thirty-two-year-old mother consulted me about such sudden and extreme outbursts of temper at her three young children that she feared she'd physically abuse them. The dread and guilt she carried on her shoulders, on top of her anger, blocked any hope she had for happiness.

So could fifty-eight-year-old Tom. A physical therapist repeatedly fired from his job because of belligerent behavior, he took umbrage at every mistake, oversight, and slight from both coworkers and clients alike. Not only was he made miserable by his own anger, but he also suffered from the misery of guilt and depression after every termination.

And I'm sure forty-nine-year-old Kate recognized herself as well. A year before she consulted with me, her husband of twenty years told her he wanted a divorce. The bitterness and rage she felt on a daily basis soiled any chance she had to rebuild her life and find happiness.

These three people – Jenny, Tom, and Kate – are but a few of my many patients who found it difficult to be happy with others. One solution to the happiness-killing anger would have been to only hang out with perfect people, people who would never cross them. Good luck with that.

A more realistic solution would be to train them to adopt the breakthrough strategy of Premeditated Acceptance and Forgiveness. This is the strategy I want you to learn, as did Jenny, Tom, and Kate. Once you do, you will be free to employ the six additional strategies to build your happiness quotient with others, which I will share later in this chapter.

Breakthrough Strategy Three: Premeditated Acceptance and Forgiveness

In this section, I will help you both understand the root source of your hurt and anger and show you how to eliminate it from your dealings with others. As you read on, please bring your full attention, openness, and commitment. With these in place, you can't help but find more happiness in your life.

The Anatomy of Hurt and Anger

Many myths abound about what causes hurt and anger. Perhaps the most pernicious one is that other people have the power to emotionally cause us to feel that way. How often do we hear it said: "She made me mad." "That hurt my feelings." "He gets under my skin."

What these statements communicate is that other people, by virtue of their thoughts and behaviors, have the power to project into us feelings of hurt and anger. We have no choice. Others act in some onerous way, which, in turn, stimulates us to reflexively react emotionally.

If there were truth to this myth, then we would all be the emotional pawns of other people. All they would have to do is treat us badly and we spin off into the throes hurt and anger. Fortunately, this is not true. Literally thousands of research studies, plus millions of case examples, prove that it is not the obnoxious behavior of others that cause these pernicious feelings, but the judgmental ways we think.

We Rational Emotive Behavior Therapy practitioners represent this with our ABC model, as illustrated in Figure 6.1. In this model, A represents the Activating Event, that is, the sin of commission or omission committed by the other person. The C stands for our Emotional Consequences of hurt and anger. Mediating between the A and the C is the B, the evaluative or Judgmental Belief about the A. This belief, the B, which we choose to hold about the A, in turn causes the C.

At its core, the ABC's is a model of emotional responsibility. While other people can, and indeed often do, treat us shabbily, they cannot make us experience emotional hurt and anger. Rather, we do this to ourselves by the way we think about what they do. The profoundly powerful implication of this is that, with effort, we can take charge of our thinking and stubbornly refuse to upset ourselves no matter how badly other people behave.

Take, for example, Bill and Bob, both of whom were the recipients of rude, dismissive behavior from their boss – the A. Bill, at B, thinks: "Well, that sure was crappy, but so what, that's just the way he is." He may then react with mild displeasure, but he gets on with his workday without suffering the poisonous effect of hurt and anger. Now, contrast him with Bob. Bob receives the same treatment from his boss as did Bill, but alternately he thinks: "How dare he treat me like that; he shouldn't do that, the damn guttersnipe." Thinking this way, he brings on himself the emotional contamination of hurt and anger. The bottom line: Both men experienced the same Activating Event (the A), but their radically different beliefs at B caused their different emotional reactions at C.

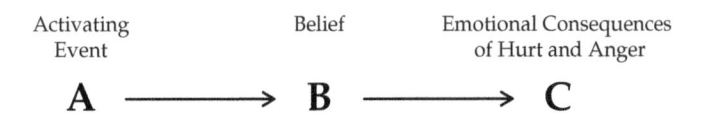

Figure 6.1 The ABCs of Hurt and Anger

The Killer Bs

So that's the Anatomy of Hurt and Anger. To start the process of eliminating these happiness-wrecking contaminants, you need to accept responsibility for causing your hurt and anger by the way you think. Then you can track down those pernicious beliefs as a prelude to eliminating them.

That's exactly what Jenny, Tom, and Kate did. With a little guidance, they discovered the belief that brought on their hurt and anger:

JENNY: When her children acted unruly (the A), her knee-jerk thought (the B) was, "Dammit, they should just settle down and mind me, the little monsters."

TOM: In response to some annoying behavior of a colleague at work (the A), he habitually thought (the B), "That idiot ought to know better than to act so stupid."

KATE: When her husband left her (the A), she adopted the attitude (the B), "I've devoted the best years of my life to him and he shouldn't have done this to me, the no-good bastard."

A careful analysis of these three peoples' beliefs reveals the three Killer Bs that caused them so much hurt and anger. What was true for these people is true for you as well.

1. Demanding Perfection

Communicated by such absolutistic words as "should," "ought," and "must," we endorse an expectation that others should never error, act badly, or cross us in any way, shape, or form. That's exactly the way Jerry, Tom, and Kate thought. Note the bitterness each brought on by demanding perfection from the people in their lives. Ask yourself if these demands are reasonable.

2. Catastrophizing

With such expressions as "awful," "horrible," and "terrible," we blow the degree of badness of another's sin of commission or omission so out of proportion that it rises to the level of a crime against humanity. To Jenny, her children not only acted annoyingly, but at the serial killer level. Likewise, Tom believed that the peccadilloes of his coworkers were despicable horrors. And Kate didn't just read her husband's decision to leave her as merely unfortunate or bad, but so monstrous that he deserved to roast in hell for at least half an eternity. See if you don't find yourself thinking along these lines whenever you feel hurt and anger.

3. Other Damning

Dr. Albert Ellis, the father of Rational Emotive Behavior Therapy, was never one to speak politically correct. He told it the way he saw it when he famously said, "Shouldhood leads to sh_ _hood." What he meant by that is that, when we demand perfection of someone, and rate their bad behavior as horrendous, we also most assuredly will damn them as monsters – in other words, as totally bad people who deserve our wrath. This one mistake, the bad thing the other person did, makes him or her a totally rotten or worthless person, just as the one rotten orange referenced in the last chapter renders the whole crate of oranges rotten and unworthy of consumption. Does such total damning of another person for one error or fault seem logical to you?

These, then, are the three core beliefs behind all hurt and anger: (1) demanding that others always act right; (2) rating their misdeeds or faults as unspeakable horrors; and, (3) damning them as atavistic throwbacks. This insight will start you on the journey to living a hurt- and anger-free life, one that opens the door to then finding persistent and powerful happiness with others. But now to the antidote.

The Antidote: Get Real

It is not surprising that we adopt these Killer Bs, for our entire socialization process trains us to expect the best and brightest from both ourselves and others. Parents insist their children keep their room clean, eat their broccoli, do their chores. Teachers demand that their students always be on time and be prepared, pay attention in class, study hard, and get good grades. The good book insists that we should honor God, adhering to His commandments. To do otherwise is to risk the wrath of our parents, teachers, and even God.

But what if we got it backward? What if we trained ourselves to think more realistically about our fellow human beings? What if we recognized their innate fallibility and expected them to blunder? What if we didn't catastrophize when they do? What if we only damned their behavior but never their personhood?

I remember one evening when my older son, Todd, was a teenager. I don't recall his exact misbehavior, but I do remember the ire I felt, the impassioned lecture I delivered, the volume of my angry voice.

He stopped me dead in my tracks when he said, "Dad, I'm sorry for what I did, but you've got to get real. I'm a teenager. I'm never going to be perfect."

That proved to be one of the seminal moments in my parenting life. It illustrated to me in quite personal terms that I drove myself, not to mention him, around the bend with my unrealistic expectations for his perfection. When I examined my self-talk, I found it to be littered with explications of "shoulds," "musts," and "ought tos," as in: "He should know better." "He ought to be more motivated in school." "He should religiously follow the rules."

Like me with my son, you'd be wise to relinquish your perfectionistic demands, your framing your compatriots' missteps as atrocities, and your damning them as despicable for their dislikable behavior. Instead, adopt the following ways of thinking:

1. Expect Imperfection

The truth is, being human and fallible, every single one of the people in your life, loved ones and casual acquaintances alike, are innately fallible and imperfect. Given that, they therefore have to, must, got to, need to, and, yes, should act badly. Furthermore, they must do so, not when it's convenient for you or with your permission, but when they do. Too bad. You may not like what they do or when they do so, but remember that you are not so special as to demand that people misbehave only when it suits you. To quote Todd, "Get real."

2. Practice Perspective

Imagine that there existed a fact-based scale of badness on which we could realistically place anything bad in our life somewhere between 1% and 100% bad. Only those things that are truly tragic – say the death of your child, the murder of over three thousand people on September 11, 2001, or a nuclear war – are so bad that deserve to be placed somewhere between 90% and 100% bad. If they stopped and thought, wouldn't Jenny, Tom, and Kate rate what they made themselves angry about somewhere between 1% and 10% bad? If they had, the worst they could have felt was annoyed, not angry. You can do this too with the annoying activating events in your life. With this perspective, be sure to rate everything that goes wrong in your life where it realistically belongs. If you force yourself to rigorously apply the scale, you will find that fully 95% of the things about which you anger yourself are less than 10% bad. Get real.

3. Damn the Behavior, Never the Person.

Just like with yourself in the last chapter, damning another person is also an illogical overgeneralization. No matter how inappropriate or wrong someone's actions may be, this obnoxious behavior neither defines the whole person nor rates him or her as all bad. He is not a rude person for acting rudely, she is not a liar for lying, they are not bad for acting badly. Get real: Apply the same unconditional acceptance to other people as well as to yourself.

From Theory to Practice

To get the most possible happiness you can from your relationship life, you have to work hard at practicing Premeditated Acceptance and Forgiveness. It requires you to get your expectations in line with reality. To help you do so, consider adopting the following five practices.

1. First thing every morning, take a few minutes to have a little chat with yourself. Remind yourself that the people with whom you will interact with that day are human. They are fallible and they are likely to misbehave at some point. Expect it. Chalk it up to their human nature. Unless it is two egregious to be ignored, let it slide.

2. When you find yourself angry or hurt by someone's misbehavior, remember that it was your demand ("He/she shouldn't have misbehaved."), not their behavior that set you off. Correct your unrealistic expectations and let go of your hurt and anger.

3. Follow the advice of hypnotherapist Milton Erickson (1976): Find the positive characteristics the people in your life possess, particularly those most significant to you – their sparkling smile, their generosity, their sense of humor, their goodness of heart, their love of cats and dogs. Be sure to focus on these rather than their mistakes and faults. Do this for one month and I promise you will find more acceptance and forgiveness, and more happiness in your relationship life.

4. Whenever you find yourself unhappy with another, instead of dwelling on his or her misbehavior, send out a mental bouquet of gratitude. When, for example, you find yourself about to say to your wife, "How could you forget to get that package to the post office!" instead focus on something about her for which you are grateful: "I sure wish she'd remembered to do that, yet she has such a loving heart."

5. Expecting misbehavior doesn't mean that you automatically accept everybody into your life. It only means that you don't block your happiness by carrying around hurt and anger. Without being interpersonally unhappy, you still would be wise to carefully choose who you hang out with. With realistic expectations about others, and without the contaminants of hurt and anger, ask yourself the following two relationship power questions to make decisions about who to befriend: (1) Do I like, love, or care about this person? (2) Is this person good for my happiness, well-being, and productivity? Even one "no" should give you pause.

Additional Happiness with Other Strategies

Happiness with others is truly a big part of overall happiness. But, as with finding happiness with yourself, you have to purposely work at it. What follows, then, are six additional strategies – three cognitive and three behavioral – to help you find and maintain happiness in your interpersonal life. Please study them and see which ones you want to integrate into your growing Happiness Action Plan in Chapter 9.

Cognitive Strategies

1. Take Nothing Personal

A few years ago, I returned home on a Friday evening, having spent the whole workweek consulting with an out-of-town company. As rewarding as the work was, the nights spent in my antiseptic motel room with the TV as my only companion left me longing for hearth and home.

Speeding homeward on the dark interstate, the radio my companion, I fantasized about the celebratory evening that lay ahead. I envisioned my wife welcoming me at the door as a conquering hero, serving me a luscious meal as if I were an honored guest, and lavishing me with adoration fit for a caliph.

Finally, I pulled in the driveway, walked into the house, and announced, "Honey, I'm home."

Standing at the stove, her back to me, Patti glanced over her shoulder and said, "Hi, Dear. How was your trip?" With that, she kept stirring the contents of the pot in front of her.

I stopped dead in my tracks, slumped my shoulders in dejection, and slunk off to my easy chair in the family room. Once there, I thought, *Well, I guess I now know how much I really mean to her,* lapsing into a full-blown pity-party.

I didn't realize it then, but I can now see that I interpreted her reaction to my return as an intentional personal rejection of me.

Before I could stew too long, Patti glided into the family room, plopped into my lap, and wrapped her arms around my neck. "Welcome home, Dear," she said. "I was at a critical point in the special meal I'm preparing for you. Now I can greet you properly." And with that, she embraced me with all the love and tenderness I could have hoped for.

You could imagine what that did to my mood. In a flash, I went from hurt to warmth, from heavy to lighthearted, from angry to loving. And, guess what, we had the luscious evening I hoped for on my ride home.

I imagine, dear reader, that you can relate to my story. I bet that you, like me, could cite many instances when you made false assumptions about the thoughts and feelings of your loved ones, friends, and colleagues, moments when you concluded that their unlikable actions were motivated against you. We call this "taking it personal."

Here's a newsflash: Whatever you do, never take what others do personally. Remember that nothing others do is because of you. It is because of them. Patti didn't tend to her cooking rather than rush into my arms in order to offend me; she did so because of the circumstances she found herself in. Even if she no longer loved me and didn't want to greet me warmly, her ceasing to love me wouldn't be against me. Her not loving me would not be personal. It would just be the way she unfortunately felt. While I might feel sad about it, I need not take it as a personal, intentional affront.

Taking nothing personal is a hard lesson to learn. We are programmed to do so. If somebody calls you a name, say "stupid" or "superficial" or "thoughtless," it's easy to think, "Of course it's personal, because he called ME that name." But his vilifying words are really more about him than you; it's about how he sees the world, about his irrational way of thinking, about the way he's put together. Even if someone hauls off and slugs you, it's not personal. I know that sounds crazy, but that behavior is about how that person is – how his personality works at that moment, with all his or her foibles and nuances, not a premeditated, plotted out, rehearsed response. And, even it was, doesn't even that reflect upon that person, not you.

Here's my advice: Never, ever, take anything anyone does personal. When you really understand that other people do what they do because of who they are, even when they act mean or nasty, you will never deeply suffer from what they say or do. You may feel sad, frustrated, or disappointed, but you will not feel hurt or angry to the core.

To help you take nothing personal, practice the following five strategies.

(1) Be alert. Recognize when you take something personal. Label it as such and view it as an opportunity to practice de-personalizing what others do.
(2) Practice. Our human mind can not only think about objects, events, and situations outside itself, but also about its own thoughts as well. So, when you find yourself taking the behavior of another personally, you can remind yourself: "That's nonsense. He did that to me because that's the way he is. It's about him, not me." By practicing this for the next one hundred days in

a row if necessary, you can habituate your mind to do just that – take nothing personally.

(3) Study Other People. Watch when they act in some inappropriate way. Ask yourself: "What is it about them that prompts them to act that way?" Remind yourself that other people rarely lay awake at night, plotting to do you or anyone else in. Rather, when they act badly, it is usually a reactive response to some distressing emotion they are feeling. In other words, it's about them.

(4) Unconditionally Accept Yourself. As discussed in length in Chapter 5: "Happiness with Yourself," this means that you detach your identity and your worth from everybody else's feelings and actions. You may not like what they do, but you, your self, are not made more or less valuable by the approval or disapproval of others. You just are … 100% human and whole, simply because you exist. By accepting yourself unconditionally, you inoculate yourself from the misery of ever taking the words and actions of others personally.

(5) Watch Yourself. When you act badly toward another person, analyze what prompted you to do so. You'll find it most always is because you simply weren't thinking clearly. Notice that your behavior was likewise more about your state of mind at the time, not a cold-blooded desire to do harm to the other person for your simple pleasure. Remind yourself that this is true of others as well.

2. Be Generous of Spirit

A couple of Decembers ago, my wife and I took our younger son to see a stage production of *A Christmas Carol*. Remember Ebenezer Scrooge? He is a grasping miser who cares only about money, shutting out all human warmth, and treating people with no compassion or concern. To him, people are only tools to help him line his pockets.

The dramatic center of this fable occurs on Christmas Eve when Scrooge is visited by three ghosts who conduct what we would today call an intervention. They force him to take an unvarnished look at his life and give him an opportunity to transform his heart.

The Ghost of Christmas Past transports Scrooge back to his youth where he sees all the family warmth and happiness he no longer has. The Ghost of Christmas Present takes him to the home of his employee, Bob Cratchit, whose family feels nothing but love for each other despite the impending death of their beloved son, Tiny Tim. The Ghost of Christmas Future takes him forward to his gravesite where no one remembers or cares that he ever lived.

Sure enough, the intervention works. Scrooge faces up to the waste and barrenness that is his life. Awakening on Christmas Day, he finds that he is still alive, a newborn man. He bounds out his front door, seeing every person he meets as an opportunity to make his or her life nicer, warmer, richer. Right before our eyes he becomes a living, breathing wellspring of generosity. Not only does he spread the gift of happiness to others, but he experiences it himself – fully and fervently.

The spirit of generosity – what a gift to give to others and to yourself! Imagine the positive impact you'd have on others with a willingness to be relentlessly generous with them. Imagine the goodwill you'd create by leaving no encounter without finding some small way to offer generosity. Imagine how happy and fulfilled you'd feel expressing this throughout your day.

I want to emphasize that, by generosity, I do not mean giving tangible things to people, though doing so might indeed be an act of generosity. It is more a gift of self. I think of a married couple I now counsel whose relationship was wrecked by conflict and ill will. Although they had learned to use sound communication skills, it was when they each adopted the spirit of generosity that their relationship began to soar. Without any instruction as to exactly what to do, they became attentive to each other, went out of their way to express affection, and overlooked or forgave the slights they once escalated into atrocities.

By adopting the spirit of generosity, you will add to the happiness in your life. But, as I've preached before, the universe will not bestow happiness on you just because you exist. To add generosity of spirit to your happiness toolkit, you must work at it. Here then are five things you can do:

1. Be aware of the opportunities. If each of us went home each evening and treated the members of our family with generosity, the world would be transformed. So, first, be aware of the opportunities with the people in your life to express generosity. As with the couple I previously mentioned, you don't need a skill-building course, just a healthy dose of awareness, along with a willingness to act accordingly.
2. Recognize the benefits to you. What you sow, so shall you reap. By acting toward others with the spirit of generosity, you will without question make a positive impression, perhaps even elicit affection, so that they will most likely be motivated to respond in kind. You now are the beneficiary of the generosity they extend back to you. Be aware of and appreciate the benefits to you, born out of your generosity to others.

3. Be proud of your generous spirit. You most likely do not have the power to transform the planet, but you can make a profound difference within your little corner of the world. Start with your immediate family, then expand to your friends and colleagues, and go from there to the chance encounters you have with the everyday people you encounter during your day. You can and will impact them by acting with this spirit of generosity. It's quite a transformative practice, so be proud of it.

4. Teach it. When we teach something to others, we tend to learn it deeper ourselves. I have to say that this is one of the great benefits my clinical psychology practice gives me; as I spread the mental health gospel to my patients, I find it easier to live it in my own life. Make a point to teach generosity of spirit to others, particularly to your children.

5. Appreciate others' generosity. One of my dear friends never fails to send a note of "thank you" for presents, after our get-togethers, and the like. In addition to appreciating these generous acts from others, remind yourself to model them yourself.

3. Don't Overcare about What Others Think

Let me tell you about a patient of mine, who I'll call Rachel. When she first walked into my office, I was immediately struck by her beauty. *I can't imagine why she's consulting a shrink*, I thought.

Well, I soon found out. Through a soft voice I had to strain to hear, with tears welling in her eyes, she told me the sad story of her relationship life, a lengthy series of disasters that followed a similar pattern, all ending in heartbreak and devastation. Each started with mutual attraction and excitement that soon aroused an urgent sense of needy desperation on her part, followed by increasing demands for more time, attention, and reassurance. Once her new beau found this clinging behavior annoying, her insecurity and neediness escalated. Inevitably a vicious circle developed: Escalating neediness on her part aroused more irritation and frustration on his, further escalating her insecurity. On and on it went until the guy eventually had enough and left her.

Sitting there sobbing, Rachel blurted out: "Dr. Grieger, the last guy told me I was repulsive. What's wrong with me?"

The answer was pretty obvious, as you've probably already figured out. What was wrong with Rachel was that she had irrationally turned a healthy desire for the pleasure of love and affection into an absolute conviction that she couldn't exist without it. By holding this belief, she acted so desperate, fearful, and needy that she eventually destroyed any chance of getting what she wanted.

That was what Rachel worked so hard in psychotherapy to change – her fervent belief that she needed, absolutely had to have, the love of a man in order to survive, have any pleasure in life, and find life worthwhile. At the time of this writing, she is starting to relinquish this misery-making way of thinking. Once she does, there is no reason why she can't have the relationship happiness she so desires.

To enhance your happiness with others, you too would be wise to live without neediness. There's nothing wrong with wanting the love and approval of others, for this desire is built into our DNA. It provides you the motivation to pursue this profound source of happiness. But, do not let yourself believe that you need it, for that will make you desperate, unhappy, and, like Rachel, unattractive.

To help you desire but never need the love and approval of others, here are five strategies you can adopt:

1. Understand the five reasons why you do not literally need the love or approval of any particular person: (1) it is not a matter of life and death – you will die without food and air, but not if he/she doesn't care; (2) if some particular person doesn't love or like you, you still retain everything else that is good in your life to enjoy – you haven't lost everything; (3) no matter who it is you value but doesn't care back for you, this person is replaceable – you can always love or like somebody else who will also love or like you; (4) it is illogical and, frankly, quite demanding, to think that, because you want this person's love, he/she must respond in kind – after all, you don't run the universe; and (5) who you are is not defined by anyone's love and approval – remember that you just are, alive and human, and will always be so till you no longer exist, with or without that person's desired affection.
2. Identify the people who you think you need to love or like you. Then, while being careful to not shut down your genuine feelings for them, avidly practice reminding yourself that, while you desire their approval, you don't absolutely need it.
3. For five minutes, three times a day – before breakfast, lunch, and dinner – reflect on why you don't need anybody's love and approval. For example, at breakfast, think of who you might encounter before lunch and then go through the reasons why you don't need their approval. Do the same again before lunch and dinner. Do this for one hundred consecutive days.
4. Imagine yourself in an upcoming real-life situation. Be as vivid as you can in picturing the people you will encounter. Then picture yourself caring, but

not overcaring or needing them to think well of you. Make this a practice before all social situations.

5. Practice Unconditional Self-Acceptance, as laid out in Chapter 5: "Happiness with Yourself." Want or don't want another's love and approval, be pleased or displeased with how they hold you, but never define or judge yourself by what they think of or feel about you. Make this a fervent practice.

Behavioral Strategies

1. Choose Friends and Lovers Wisely

Let me remind you of a sobering fact. You have a finite amount of time in your life. An average lifetime of 75.5 years equals roughly 2.4 billion seconds, a fraction of the wealth accumulated by Warren Buffett. So, you would be wise to squeeze as many positives into your life as you can, as well as eliminating as many negatives as possible.

This applies especially to your relationships life. Sadly, all too often, I work with people who have contaminated their happiness by befriending people who are not good for them. Worse, even after finding these people to be pernicious, they frequently continue the relationship.

Take, for example, fifty-three-year-old Sally. Her toxic relationship is with her mother. This mother has a history of being critical of Sally, sometimes even resorting to physical violence. As a result, Sally struggled with issues of self-worth, fears of disapproval, and depression, for as long as she can remember. Her first chore in therapy focused on disconnecting her worth from her mother's approval, and repairing her sense of self. Chore two focused on helping Sally decide whether or not to continue this toxic relationship. What do you think would be the best thing for her to do?

Bob presents another example. Married to a woman whose anger outbursts are as volcanic as they are frequent, he is reluctant to throw in the towel after some forty years of marriage. Assuming this woman is not going to change, the question he would be wise to consider is: Are the benefits of this relationship worth the cost?

Then there's Helen. Forty-two years old and childless, she has been dating a man for five years who wants to marry her. She feels comfortable with him, yet feels little passion and wonders if he has what it takes to stimulate both her sense of humor and her intellect. She is torn about what to do: Should I or should I not make a lifelong commitment to him?

There's a metaphor I use to empower my patients to make sound relationship decisions that I call "The Grocery Store." I ask them to first think of themselves as the product sitting on the shelf, say a can of soup. They rest there, desperately hoping to be purchased, but having little or no choice in the matter. With this mentality, they leave the store with anybody who will put them in their basket and take them to the cash register. Then I ask them to picture themselves being the shopper – walking the aisle, consciously checking out the ingredients on each can's label to see if they're nutritious and tasty, and only purchasing the one that fits the bill.

I urge you to adopt this shopper mentality. To help you do so, I offer you five strategies to help you choose your lovers and friends wisely.

(1) Conduct an honest inventory. Scan the people in your life. These could be intimate others, family members, friends, work colleagues, or even relatively minor acquaintances. Regardless, honestly note those relationships that are fraught with difficulty, ones that pose for you the same type of dilemmas faced by Sally, Bob, and Helen. By identifying such people, you are now positioned to be the shopper rather than the can of soup.

(2) Shed your fear. Understand that fear can block you from confronting or ridding difficult and/or toxic people from your life. Search out and destroy the flawed logic that creates these fears: (1) fears of disapproval – "This person must not be upset with me."; (2) fears of making a mistake – "I must make the right decision."; (3) fears of discomfort – "I must not experience the discomfort of dealing with this person or this situation." Getting rid of your fears will free you to shop wisely.

(3) Answer what I call the two power questions to decide whether or not to enter into or continue with a relationship: (1) Do I like, care about, love, or in some ways find value in this person? If the answer is "no" to this question, then either rid this person from your life or minimize your contact with him or her. (2) Is this person good for me? If the answer to this second question is "no," then also rid this person from your life, even if the answer to the first question might be a "yes." After all, we can like or care about all kinds of difficult, even destructive people. None of this precludes, of course, holding a heart-to-heart with this difficult person, explaining the problems his or her behavior pose for you, and letting the person know you will only continue the relationship if things change. Then it's in the other person's court as you wait and see if changes are made.

(4) Refuse to feel guilty. Do not guilt-trip yourself about the decision to not enter into or terminate a relationship with someone you find toxic. There is no universal imperative that commands you to be in or stay in a relationship

with any particular person, nor is your judgment that it is not in your best interest to connect with someone a selfish thing. Your responsibility is first and foremost to yourself, regardless what the other person wants from you.

(5) Water and fertilize your good relationships. Once you have shopped wisely, put energy into making the relationships you've chosen as vibrant and rewarding as possible.

2. Be a Relentless Giver

Legend has it that during the recording of the Beatles' legendary *White Album*, Ringo Starr quit the band because he felt unappreciated. Here's what he said: "I went to see John, who had been living in my apartment in Montague Square with Yoko since he moved out of Kenwood. I said: 'I'm leaving the group because I feel unloved and out of it.'"

So, how did it work out? Let's turn to the sage psychologist, Paul McCartney, for the answer (2000):

> I think Ringo was always paranoid that he wasn't a great drummer. But, I think his feel and soul and the way he was rock solid with his tempo was a good attribute.
>
> You could just tell Ringo how it went and leave him – there was always this great noise and steady tempo coming from behind you.... So at that time we had to reassure him that we did think he was great.
>
> That's what it's like in life. You go through life and you never stop and say, 'Hey, you know what? I think you're great.' You don't always tell your favorite drummer that he's your favorite drummer. Ringo felt insecure and he left, so we told him, 'Look man, you are the best drummer in the world to us.' He said, 'Thank you,' and I think he was pleased to hear it. We ordered millions of flowers and there was a big celebration to welcome him back to the studio.

Wise words indeed. Everybody loves affection and appreciation. Who doesn't puff up, when made to feel significant, affirmed, and acknowledged? It warms the heart, nourishes the soul.

But here's an extra-added benefit. We gain as much from giving to others as do those to whom we give. How so? Well, in two ways. One, there can be real pleasure and joy in the act of giving. It simply feels good to be good to others, especially when we do so with a spirit of generosity. Try it and see if I'm not right. Two, people remember how you make them feel long after they forget what you said to them. So, by being a giver, people are likely to hold good feelings about you and then return your giving in kind.

The bottom line is that, by being a relentless giver to others, you can double your own happiness. All of us would be wise to build in acts of giving in our daily interaction with others. To help you along the path, here are five daily practices. Try them and see if you don't get pleasure from them. See if the people you give to don't respond in kind. See if the pleasures from your relationships increase.

(1) Give compliments. This is easy. You can always find something positive to compliment when you encounter another – "You look good in that color." "Your lawn looks great." "That was an interesting thing you just said." It's the hunger for these kinds of strokes that make people feel good about you and want to be a giver to you in return.

(2) Say "Thank you" often. People appreciate being appreciated. "Thank yous" can be communicated verbally, by letter, by email. Regardless, they mean a lot. And, here's a tip: Little "thank yous" count too. I appreciate it almost as much when my wife thanks me for picking up our son from the skate park as I do when she tells me how much she appreciates how hard I work to help support our family.

(3) Treat people with kindness. With people, little things are the big things. Every time we act in a kind way, no matter how small it may be, we invite them to act kindly to us in return. Kindness is the happiness gift that keeps on giving.

(4) Express compassion. Compassion is perhaps the greatest gift one can give to another. When one is hurting, it does wonders to hear, "I'm sorry you're going through this," "I care for you," "I'm here for you." It feels good to comfort another and it builds the bonds of friendship that nourishes our own happiness as well.

(5) Touch often. True, there are some people who are squeamish about being touched. They find these gestures too intimate to handle. But, the vast majority of people enjoy a good old-fashioned squeeze of the hand, a pat on the back, an affectionate hug. While being careful not to offend someone who might be made uncomfortable by being touched, a friendly, affectionate touch can both give and get pleasure.

3. Listen, Listen, Listen

Imagine yourself sitting comfortably in a lounge chair, a blanket over your lap. Outside your picture window is a beautiful lake, framed by tall trees floating their gold and red leaves to the ground, the setting sun rippling sparkles to the shore. Soft, yet rich music plays in the background as a crackling fire keeps you cozy and snug.

As you sit there, peaceful and serene, you start to find it hard to breathe. You gasp for air, but your lungs don't fill. You're suffocating. Panic sets in. The fear that you may die blocks out the music, the autumn splendor, the warming fire. Nothing matters except filling your lungs with air.

So, what's the point? To borrow from Stephen Covey (1989), the author of *The 7 Habits of Highly Effective People*, being listened to is the psychological equivalent of air. It is the deepest hunger of the human heart. It communicates to another: "You matter to me, I find you of value, I care for and respect you." It nourishes the spirit, stimulates affection, solidifies bonds, and adds to human happiness.

I experienced the rewards of being listened to just recently. At a wedding reception, my wife's brother, Joe, a man I already liked and respected, sidled up next to me and asked, "What's this I hear about you writing another book?"

He looked me in the eye and listened as I blathered on. He then peppered me with questions about what motivates me to work as hard as I do, what, if any plans I had for retirement, what advice I might have for him. All the while, he gave me his full attention.

I loved being the center of his attention. More importantly, I left the conversation feeling connected to Joe, more willing to reciprocate his interest in kind, primed to do my part to build a relationship that would add to both our life's happiness.

I'm sure you've had similar experiences. What I felt is what others feel when they feel heard. Being affirmed in this way, you become motivated to reciprocate. Listening spreads happiness, which rebounds back to you like a basketball.

To master listening, you must practice and practice until it becomes a habit. Consider integrating the following five strategies into your daily relationship life:

1. Get motivated. Think of five times when someone did not listen to you. How did it feel? Was it warm and fuzzy, or frustrating and annoying? How did it affect your relationship with this person going forward? Think about it. Knowing the costs of not listening can motivate you to practice getting better at it.

2. Apply it. Identify those relationships in which you would be wise to listen. Then do an inventory: What is your usual approach to these people? How often and how deeply do you listen? What happens to the quality of these relationships when you don't bother to listen? What will you do the next time when you're with these people?

3. Practice. Once a day, practice listening to another person. There are five levels of listening you can use: (1) just button your lip, look the other person in the eye, and pay attention; (2) do all the above, plus nod and give verbal affirmations: "Uh, huh;" "okay;" "yeah."; (3) listen carefully to the ideas expressed, sum them up in your own words and paraphrase them back to the person (for example, "So, Bob, what you're saying is that Obamacare is the best (worst) piece of legislation you've ever seen."); (4) listen carefully to the feelings expressed, capture them in your own words, and feed them back (as per, "You sound really disgusted (thrilled) with that piece of legislation."); (5) listen carefully to both the ideas and the feelings the person expresses, gather both together in your mind, and feed them back to the person in your own words. (e.g., "So, Bob, you really are upset (thrilled) with Obamacare because you think it is the most destructive (wonderful) piece of legislature ever."). Keep up your practice for a month and watch yourself grow stronger at it.

4. Teach it. One of the best ways to learn something is to teach it to others. Teach your kids, your significant other, and anyone else you can find the ins-and-outs of listening. Then practice it with them.

5. Eliminate barriers. Several things make it difficult to listen. Among the more common ones are emotional arousal, ego, and impatience. When you are upset, or think you are so important that people must listen to you, or find it difficult to take the time, listening becomes impossible. Do any of these barriers apply to you? If so, be aware of when they become activated so you can consciously override them and listen.

Your Happiness with Others Action Plan

Don't forget that your happiness is your own responsibility – no one else's. In that spirit, here is an opportunity to think about how you might translate the concepts and skills I presented in this chapter into action. You can put them into practice now, or you can earmark those you want to include in the Happiness Action Plan you will finally in Chapter 9. Either way, give this your best thought, as if your happiness depends on it.

Prompt One: Practicing Premeditated Acceptance and Forgiveness. Select two strategies from those discussed on pages 13–15 to help you eliminate the happiness-destroying emotions of hurt and anger from your life. For each, consider exactly what you will do and when and where you'll do it.

	Strategy	What	Where/When
1.	_____	_____	_____
	_____	_____	_____
2.	_____	_____	_____
	_____	_____	_____

Prompt Two: Additional Happiness with Other Strategies. Select two additional happiness with other strategies that you think will would elevate your life's happiness. As before, determine exactly what you will do to actualize that strategy in your life and where and when you will do it.

	Strategy	What	Where/When
1.	_____	_____	_____
	_____	_____	_____
2.	_____	_____	_____
	_____	_____	_____

Going Forward

Congratulations on a job well done. Along with your passionate purpose and your efforts to be happy with yourself, you now have strategies to find more happiness with the others in your life. Whether you take a pause here now to engrain these new strategies into your life, or you want to immediately forge forward in this book, I look forward to meeting up with you in the next chapter, *Happiness with Life*. See you there.

Notes

7

HAPPINESS WITH LIFE

Most patients who seek my clinical help do so when dealing with some sort of adversity. Many of these are relatively minor – a failed course, a suspended driver's license, an illness that causes the cancellation of a vacation trip. Others are more serious, ranging from a broken marriage to a crippling illness.

While all these adversities rate as bad, the common denominator that brings these people to my office is that they judge their adversities to be so horrible that they are life destroying. By catastrophizing their hardships, they cause themselves to experience such forms of unhappiness as depression, bitterness, and panic, emotional states that often rival in severity the original adversity itself.

Three of my current patients illustrate the ravages of catastrophizing. Consider twenty-one-year-old Glen. Bright, handsome, and athletic, he told the story of being relentlessly bullied by his elementary school classmates. Not only did he suffer their indignities, but he also concluded that the world was such an awful, unbearable place to live in that it offered no chance for happiness. This perspective hardened over time until he became so depressed that he saw suicide as a viable option.

Then there's forty-seven-year-old Ellen. After discovering that her husband had an affair, she became racked with anxiety that he might repeat this betrayal. After some probing, I learned that she believed that it would be so terrible to go through that trauma again that she absolutely couldn't bear it.

I lastly share the story of sixty-eight-year-old William. A chronic catastrophizer, he looked upon every adversity, no matter how trivial or inconsequential, as an insufferable horror that destroys the very fabric of his life. The final straw that drove him into my office, brimming with bitterness and despair, was a financial setback that necessitated that he and his wife move to a smaller, less expensive dwelling. More about him later.

Notice that Glen, Ellen, and William shared three things in common. First, they each faced a significant adversity that would present a challenge to anyone. Two, they each concluded that their adversity was so horrible that it rendered their life unbearable. Third, they each suffered such emotional misery that they found it impossible to experience any happiness as a result of their catastrophizing.

As with all my patients, I hold two goals as paramount. First of all, I try to help them think more realistically about their current adversities. That is, I want to convince them that their adversity, while bad, is more in the order of a hassle or hardship, not some totally life-ruining horror. If I succeed in this, they can not only find relief from their current misery, but they can also strive unencumbered for happiness.

Second, I try to unhappiness-proof them for the rest of their lives. I do this by helping them learn to live by the breakthrough strategy of Perspective. By which I mean that it is important for their happiness to only gauge future adversities as unfortunate, not so horrible that it ruins the rest of their life. In fact, I stress that there is nothing that is horrible in the universe.

"What?" I can almost hear you shout. "That's ridiculous. There are indeed horribles in life, things that are truly awful, which ought to make us feel depressed, bitter, and anxious. To react otherwise would be inhuman."

And I say to you in return, please open your mind. Be willing to challenge that premise. Let me convince you that, if you rigorously apply logic, you can accept that there are few if any catastrophes in life, that you can keep your life's hardships in perspective, and that you can, as long as you think rigorously, eliminate almost all your unhappinesses. Then, with this breakthrough strategy of Perspective in place, you can go about using the additional strategies in this book to build a happy life.

Breakthrough Strategy Four: Keeping All Adversity in Perspective

Here then is an opportunity to learn how to rarely, if ever, fall into the pit of emotional misery about the vicissitudes in your life. Please be totally open. Remember that, as a windsurfer, you can't always control the wind, the waves, or the weather, but you can always enjoy the ride.

Learning from William

Remember that William brought himself to therapy because of bitterness and depression about his having to move from the house he dearly loved to a smaller dwelling. Witness the conversation we had in his second psychotherapy session that started him on the road to recovery.

DR. G.: So, William, we already know that your *horriblizing* about selling your home brings on your depression. If you want to feel better, you'll have to change that type of thinking.

WILLIAM: But it is horrible. I love that house.

DR. G.: I know you do. But, let me play Socrates for a minute and ask you some questions. Your job is to answer them with logic, not emotion. Okay?

WILLIAM: Okay.

DR. G.: So, then, let's imagine a scale of badness. On this scale, something can rate as anywhere from one percent bad, say a headache, to one hundred percent bad, like the murder of your children. Now, with your two sons' death ranking all the way to the top, how would you rate your moving to a smaller home? Force yourself to be objective, as would a scientist.

WILLIAM: Since you put it that way, I guess it would be about a twenty.

DR. G.: Right, it's undesirable or bad, but somewhere much closer to the bottom of the scale than the top. It sure doesn't belong at the top of the scale where you put it, does it? So it's not a horror to have to move, just a hardship. With this perspective, rather than thinking of it as horrible, what would be a more accurate term?

WILLIAM: I don't know, maybe crummy?

DR. G.: Exactly. Now, if you'd change your thinking from "This is so horrible I can't bear it," to "It sucks, but it's not the end of the world," how would you then feel instead of bitter and depressed?

WILLIAM: I guess frustrated, maybe sad.

DR. G.: Right, but not depressed. Now, let me ask you a few more questions to really nail the fact that moving to a smaller home, while crummy, is not the depression-producing horror you've made it out to be. First, does moving into a smaller, less desirable home ruin everything in your life?

WILLIAM: Of course not.

DR. G.: Right, now, second, is your life totally ruined forever by this one setback?

WILLIAM: No, it's not.

DR. G.: All right. Now, lastly, is there any reason why you should be spared from this or any other disappointment? Are you a special case, whereby setbacks like this should happen to other people, but not you?

WILLIAM: I get it.

Dr. G.: Excellent. Now, let me make two points. One, if you go over and over this perspective many times, it will soon sink in. You will realize that this turn of events is not a horror that ruins your life now and forever. Two, if you apply this perspective across the breadth of your life, you will basically rid yourself of all your depression forever.

I am happy to report that William took our conversation to heart. As he continues to retrain his thinking, he slowly but surely loosens the grip his catastrophizing has on him, thereby gradually losing his emotional misery. With that case study in mind, let's now look at what you too can learn about catastrophizing – awfulizing, horriblizing, and terriblizing – that can help you to not be miserable about any adversity you face.

1. Catastrophizing Blow Badess Way Out of Proportion

When you think that some adversity is awful, horrible, or terrible, you do not merely mean that it is unfortunate, troublesome, or bad. No, you mean that it's at the very top of the badness scale – 100% bad. You may protest, "No, I don't mean that." But, if you're honest, you'll admit that you really do. In your mind, that adversity has reached the level of 100% bad.

The fact is, though, that it is impossible for anything to reach 100% bad. Why? Because, theoretically, it could always be worse. That child could have died a year earlier. One more person could have died on 9/11. Another child abuse case could have occurred last month. Beyond that logical point, though, is a more practical one: Most every one of our so-called catastrophes don't even come close to 100% bad. If we were to rate the senseless death of three thousand innocent people on 9/11 at 100% bad, doesn't the necessity to downsize where William lives realistically fall well below that? In fact, if you think about it, fully 99.9% of the bad things we face in life fall below the level of 20% bad.

2. Catastrophizing Represents Magical Thinking

If you think about it, 100% is all there can be of anything. An athlete can only put out 100% effort, no more. A person can only love someone 100%, not 110%. A student can at best bring 100% motivation to schoolwork, not 120%. One hundred percent of anything is all there is.

Similarly, any adversity that you may face can be no worse than some degree of bad – somewhere between 1% and 100% bad. For something to be awful, horrible, terrible, it must start after bad ends – at 101% bad or more. But that's impossible. So, awful, horrible, and terrible are magical concepts that cannot exist. Avoid thinking this way at all costs.

3. Catastrophizing Communicates That Everything Is and Always Will Be Bad

To think that some adversity is awful communicates that this one bad thing that has happened in your life is so bad it ruins your entire life, not just now, but forever. So, if you've lost your house, then you've also automatically lost everything, so that there is and never will be anything good left in your life. But the truth is that, while this loss is indeed bad, you have not lost everything. You still have your family, your friends, your hobbies, your interests, your health, your intellect, your skills, and your future. So, losing your house isn't horrible. It's just bad, and most all of the rest of the good in your life still exists.

4. Catastrophizing Implies Understandability

Contained in catastrophizing is the concept of "I can't stand it." But this thought is utter nonsense. As difficult and painful as some adversity may be, it is always standable. Taken literally, the only thing that is truly unstandable is something that kills you. Furthermore, telling yourself that an adversity is unstandable just inflames your emotions, creating more upset, and invites you to further indulge the thought that the event itself is unstandable.

5. Catastrophizing Communicates That Your Life Must Be Perfectly Free of Adversity

When you judge that some adversity is awful, horrible, or terrible, you also mean that it shouldn't exist. You think: "Since it's an absolute horror to be rejected by my wife, it shouldn't happen to me." "It's awful to have had that heart attack and therefore I shouldn't have suffered it." "Child abuse is so terrible it shouldn't exist."

It is tempting to harbor these "Shoulds." But it doesn't logically follow that, because something is bad, it shouldn't exist. The reality is that it does exist, even though it may be undesirable, bad, and even reprehensible. After all, when all the conditions necessary for something to exist are present, and when none of the conditions to prevent it are present, then it must, or should, exist. Instead of railing against it, we'd be wise, then, to work to either gracefully lump it or actively change it.

6. Catastrophizing Is Self-Defeating

To think of some adversity as awful, horrible, or terrible will cause you to react with one or more of the major forms of human misery – depression, anxiety, anger, or guilt. So, you will not only have to deal with the adversity itself, but also have to deal with your own emotional unhappiness. How silly to do this to yourself. Furthermore, by creating so much misery, you will make it harder to bring a clear, calm mind to problem solving the original adversity.

All of the above is what William strives to digest. To the extent that he does, he will experience such appropriate feelings as sadness, frustration, concern, displeasure, and regret, but not the anguishes noted above. Now let's pick up again with William a little later in our conversation....

DR. G.: Good job, William. You're now decimating the idea that the loss of your home is an unbearable horror that ruins your life now and forever. The more you do, the less unhappy you'll feel. But we need to go two steps further. First, let's replace your horriblizing thoughts with ones with the proper perspective. Then we'll start figuring out what to do to build back your happiness. For now, what would be a better way to think about the loss that won't lead you down the path of emotional misery?

WILLIAM: I don't know. Maybe something like, "I don't like it, but it's not the end of the world as I know it. I have so much to be thankful for besides this. Let's get on with it."

DR. G.: Great! Now go over that every day until it sinks in. Finally, let's brainstorm a little to see what you can do to bring a little fun and pleasure in your life now that you're shedding your unhappiness. Okay?

WILLIAM: Yes!

Prompt: Self-Application. Now let's apply this to your life. Identify below some adversity in your life that you let undercut your happiness. It could be minor or major, it doesn't matter, so long as you overreacted emotionally to it. Note first what was the Activating Event (the A), then write down the unhappy feelings you had about it (the C). Most importantly, put in sentence form what was the catastrophizing thought (the B) you had that caused this feeling (e.g., William thought, "It is so horrible to lose this house I can't stand it.").

A = The Adversity:

_____

_____

B = My Irrational Catastrophizing Belief (put this in sentence form):

_____

_____

C = My Emotional Consequence:

Good. Now play Socrates with yourself. Write down as many arguments as you can to dispute the validity of your catastrophizing belief (the D, or the Disputation). You might want to refer to the seven arguments I presented above in doing this. To conclude the exercise, formulate a new effective belief (the E) that puts the degree of badness of the adversity in its proper perspective.

D = My Logical Disputation of the Catastrophizing Belief:

E = My New Effective Perspective Thinking:

Sear This into Your Mind

- Everyone will experience adversities in life. No one is exempt or immune.
- Adversities do not destroy happiness. Though frustration, disappointment and sadness naturally and appropriately result from them, depression, anxiety, and bitterness do not. These come from your catastrophizing about the adversities.
- Awful, horrible, and terrible are magical concepts that are illogical, unprovable, and debilitating. They mistakenly communicate to us that the adversities we face are 100% bad, or worse (which they aren't), ruin everything in life (which they don't), make everything in life forever bad (which, again, they don't), shouldn't exist (despite the fact that they do), and climb into the magical realm of 101% or more bad (which is impossible).

From Theory to Practice

I hope by now I've convinced you about the foolhardiness of catastrophizing. If so, you might want to devote yourself to the following five practices, all of which can reduce your unhappiness and enhance your happiness.

1. Become clear about the distinction between bad and horrible. Bad refers to something undesirable and can rate anywhere from 1% to 100% negative.

But, in fact, very few things rate worse than 20% bad, and nothing can rise to the level of 100% bad, ruin everything in life, and be unstandable. Awful, horrible, and terrible mean the opposite: They mean that this adversity is 100% or more bad, it ruins everything in life, now and forever, it's unstandable, and it shouldn't exist.

2. Make a list of the adversities in your life. On a scale from 1 to 100, determine – exactly and precisely, as would a scientist – the degree of badness this adversity actually represents. Be intellectually rigorous as you do this, refusing to succumb to emotion. See that your adversities, while bad, don't ruin your life.

3. Remember that you can stand anything. You may not like it, but it is always standable. Give up this nonsensical way of thinking.

4. Count your blessings. Without denying the existence of your adversities, also see all the good that is in your life, blessings you can enjoy while you rue the adversities.

5. Look to the future. What can you create in your life that can give you pleasure and happiness, even though your adversities may endure? List these and work toward them. This is the focus of the next section of this chapter. Read on.

Additional Happiness with Life Strategies

A colleague of mine once remarked, "We cannot prevent wasps from flying over our heads, but we can sure keep them from building a nest in our hair." Analogously, there's no way we can live a life free of hardships and hassles, but we can be sure to keep them in perspective, thereby keeping depression, bitterness, and anxiety at bay. Now, without these type of unhappinesses, we can employ the following six strategies – three cognitive and three behavioral – to bring ourselves loads of happiness.

Cognitive Strategies

1. Reject Victimhood

I'll never forget Sabrina. When she walked into my office one cold December evening, she looked so frail I swore I could have knocked her over with a feather. In the section of her intake papers labeled "Major Problems for Which You Want Help," she wrote: "Severely depressed and suicidal."

Through sobs, Sabrina told her tragic story. She grew up with an alcoholic father who terrorized her mother, brother, and herself. Verbal abuse when he was sober escalated into physical beatings when he stumbled home drunk. The three of them formed an impenetrable bond, one that insulated them emotionally from his onslaught. Thankfully, one day her father disappeared to never be heard from again.

Life changed for the better from that day forward, until, that is, about a year before I met Sabrina. That was when her mother was diagnosed with cancer and passed away within six months. At about this time, Sabrina's brother lost control of his motorcycle, slammed into a tree, and also died.

I realized I had to work fast. After expressing my sympathy, I asked Sabrina if she'd be willing to trust me enough to participate in a thought experiment. When she gave the go-ahead, I began.

DR. G: Sabrina, how many people here in Virginia do you think also suffer tragedies?

SABRINA: Many.

DR. G: What's percentage would you think? Just take a guess.

SABRINA: Maybe twenty.

DR. G: Okay. How about in our county?

SABRINA: Again, twenty.

DR. G: I agree. Now, how about in your neighborhood?

SABRINA: At least some.

I admired Sabrina's courage and pluck but paused to ask if she was doing okay. After she nodded yes, I pushed forward.

DR. G: Okay, Sabrina, I know this sounds uncaring, but what do you think I'm driving at?

SABRINA: You're trying to get me to see that I'm being selfish.

DR. G: No, I would never think you're selfish, nor would I want you to think that of yourself. Try again.

SABRINA: That I'm thinking I'm special.

DR. G: Tell me what you mean by that.

SABRINA: I'm feeling sorry for myself, thinking that this shouldn't have happened to me.

DR. G: Yes! Look, Sabrina, you've been through an awful lot – one tragic blow after another. Anybody would be reeling. I know I would. But if you let yourself rail against the universe and fall into a virulent case of self-pity – become a victim – you'll stay depressed, like you are now.

You see, we can divide people into two categories. In one category are those who whine, complain, and feel sorry for themselves when they face adversity. Instead of accepting that it is their responsibility to make the best of trying times, they think themselves the helpless, hapless victim of their life's challenging circumstances – "This is horrible. I don't deserve this. It's not fair. Poor me." They think it's life's responsibility to make their lives work. And, they descend into the emotional swamp of depression and/or bitterness.

In the second category are those who accept reality. They recognize that they are not privileged wherein adversity may strike others but not them. When they face hardships, they cope, not mope. They determine to make themselves happy, despite their difficult circumstances.

Sabrina embraced her therapy. Within months, she clawed her way out of depression and adopted a take-charge attitude. One day, she said to me: "What happened has happened. I can either buckle under and rage, or I can accept reality for what it is and do what I can to make my life better." Upon hearing these words, I knew Sabrina had completed her treatment.

To help you live a healthy life, think about adding the following perspectives to your Happiness Action Plan:

(1) Remember that, while you are special to you, as you should be, you are not a special case in the universe. Like everyone else, you will face adversities, many small and annoying, a few large and cumbersome. You have little choice in the matter. Railing against this fact will only serve to emotionally distress you. Accept it and get on with the business of improving your situation and being happy despite it.

(2) Let go of the fairness myth, as in, "That's not fair." There is no fairness czar who keeps an eye on adversities and sees to it that they are doled out equitably. Everything, good and bad, is exactly as it is, when it is. That's reality. Protesting that it's not fair only serves to destroy your happiness, adding an emotional problem on top of a practical one!

(3) Convince yourself that you can stand any adversity you face. You have stood every painful event from your past, you are probably standing some now, and you can stand whatever you face in the future. No matter what it is, you will, like Sabrina, outlive it and get on with life on the other side.

(4) Remember that, while you may not have a choice with regard to the adversities themselves, you always have a choice as to how you respond to them. This choice will greatly affect your happiness in life. You can take the victim

mentality, thinking that circumstances should always line up in your favor, thereby feeling helpless and bitter when things do not work the way you want. Or, you can adopt the belief that your life is your responsibility and determine to do what's necessary to bring yourself happiness despite any adverse circumstances that may befall you. These are your only two choices. So, choose purposefully and consciously between these two. Your happiness depends on which you choose.

(5) With the conviction that your happiness is your responsibility, determine to do whatever is necessary – within, of course, the boundaries of ethics, morals, the law, and common sense – to bring happiness to your life, no matter what.

2. Gracefully Lump Your Feel Bads

One of my dearest friends recently passed away after a long battle with cancer. I was more than honored when his wife, whom I met when they were on their first date, called and asked if there was anything I could suggest to help her cope with her loss.

I paused, not wanting to trivialize her suffering with psychobabble. After some deliberation, I suggested two things, neither being a quick fix and both requiring some follow-up coaching. A first was to honor her feelings of grief, but to also work to prevent or eliminate any depression by ridding all vestiges of irrational thinking. The second was to work to gracefully accept her painful feelings of grief, believing that they were healthy and appropriate, and trusting they would abate over time.

You see, many people upset themselves over their upsets, thereby creating a secondary emotional problem on top of their primary one. They guilt trip themselves about their anger. They react with depression about being depressed. They get anxious, even terrified, about their anxiety. They then struggle with two emotional problems for the price of one. This not only compounds their misery, but it also makes it twice as hard to find happiness.

As I write this, I think of one of my current patients. He presented severe depression that debilitated his motivation, energy, and libido, not to mention rendering him miserable. On top of that, he roundly condemned himself for his condition, thereby creating guilt for himself. He thought: "I shouldn't be so weak. I'm letting my family down. What a loser I am!"

What I want for you, dear reader, is to stubbornly refuse to go bargain-basement shopping for downers. That is, I want you to learn how to not upset yourself about being upset – to gracefully lump your feel bads, and then to get on with the business of creating happiness for yourself. Here, then, are five strategies you can use to gracefully lump the inevitable feel bads you will experience in life. Remember: It is insane to get upset about being upset, for this only compounds your upset and leads to nothing constructive.

(1) Get real. Remember that there will be regular breakdowns in your life and you will likely feel upset of one kind or another when you face them – frustration, annoyance, sadness, and/or regret, to be sure, but also anger, depression, guilt, and/or anxiety, at least sometimes. When you do, follow the old adage: "Have it (without catastrophizing) and it won't have you."

(2) Don't whine. Whining is a special form of "I'm special." When you whine, you communicate to yourself that you, being a special case in the universe, shouldn't ever experience feel bads. Nonsense! Of course, you are not so special such that you should always feel happy. Of course, you should (statistically speaking, that is) suffer at times like the rest of us.

(3) Seek out pleasure. Often when people are upset, they shut down. They pull down the shades, take the phone off the hook, and cover themselves with blankets. All this encourages brooding. Better to take charge and seek out comfort and pleasure – get in the hot tub, listen to music, go to the movies, cuddle with a loved one, make yourself a banana split. One of my patients made a long list of pleasurable activities from which to select when feeling down. Perhaps it would be a good idea for you to do this as well.

(4) Count your blessings. Nobody in their right mind wants to feel unhappy. Yet, like with the flu, it's easy to get caught up in unhappiness so that all the good in life gets ignored. Make it a practice to start off each day by reviewing the good in your life. Furthermore, when you are upset is perhaps as important a time as any to review what is good in your life – your loved ones and friends, your hobbies and interests, your creature comforts.

(5) Connect and give. What better way to get outside your own unhappiness than to reach out to others. Sharing in the warmth of friendship can balm almost any pain. Even better, focus on showing others affection, being interested in their life, helping them have a better day. This can not only get you outside of your own misery, but also can give you pleasure in and of itself.

3. Practice Gratitude

Forty-two-year-old Marsha plopped down on the couch in my clinical office. Slightly overweight, but dressed in a fashionable business suit, she looked anything but the depressed person she described herself to be on her intake sheet.

But it didn't take me long to find out why. Contrary to many people who report depression, she did not have a history of child abuse or significant failure, nor did she experience current trauma in her life. What she did reveal, though, was a steady stream of negative thinking, complaining about everything from the state of the economy to the frustrations in her job to the inclement weather outside. The picture she presented was that of a shopper in a giant clothing store who only saw nothing but ugly clothes that did not fit.

It turned out that Marsha habitually focused on the negative in her life, while, at the same time, ignoring the good. Those drove her mood lower and lower. My chore, and hers, was to break this habit and develop an attitude of gratitude.

You see, the focus of our mind matters. Why? Because, among other things, it largely determines our mood. Try focusing on everything negative in you in your life for one week and watch your mood sink. Then, for the next week, focus on nothing but the positive in your life and watch your mood elevate.

So, what we chose to focus on has the power to greatly enhance or debilitate our happiness. But, here's the good news: Our mind is like a muscle. We can train it to see and appreciate the positives, while taking care not to ignore the negatives so that we can improve on them if important.

Marsha proved to be a tough nut to crack. She initially approached her therapy with the same negativity she did with everything else in her life. "Yeah, but…." seemed to be her favorite expression. But I persisted in pointing out the steady stream of negativity that came out of her mouth and helped her see how this habit debilitated her mood, diminished her motivation, and even demoralized those around her. After weeks of struggle, she started working to rehabituate her mental focus and slowly but surely saw her depression lift and her happiness rise.

But, let me take you to the next level of focus. Being aware of what's good in life is one thing, but being grateful for what is good is another. You can certainly increase your happiness by focusing on the positive, but you can juice it even higher by being truly appreciative for the blessings you have.

Here are five strategies to help you practice gratitude, thereby bringing more happiness to your life.

(1) Set the tone. First thing each morning, review what it is in your life for which you are most grateful. Ask yourself: What is good in my life right now? What do I have to be thankful for? Who do I love who also loves me? What are the opportunities I have this day for enjoyment, pleasure, and fun? What are

the possibilities that exist to do something good or helpful? By focusing on these questions, you can set the happiness tone for the day.

(2) Be alert for the good. My wife and I watched a movie the other night titled *About Time.* The hook of the movie was a secret the father shared with his son on his twenty-first birthday. It seems that the males in the family could travel back in time. The young man did so throughout the movie to win the woman of his dreams, to save his sister from a life of drugs, and to help his best friend realize a successful career. Shortly before his death, the father told him a second secret, the secret to happiness. It was to first live each day exactly as it unfolds, then, secondly, to go back in time and relive the day, but this time paying close attention to the beautiful little things that were ignored the first time around. Of course, you cannot actually relive each day. But imagine the pleasure you could derive if you did this in the one-and-only go-around you have.

(3) Embrace good fortune. Albert Einstein once remarked: "There are two ways to live your life. One is as though nothing is a miracle. The other is as though everything is a miracle." I know that he spoke metaphorically, but I also know that, when good fortune comes your way, you can go beyond merely accepting it to celebrating it, relishing it, embracing it. This way you not only enjoy your good fortune, but you both enhance it and maximize your enjoyment of it.

(4) Embrace death. I know this sounds crazy, but the fact that death looms in front of all of us can be our biggest blessing. For our certain death can be a reminder that this is the one and only life we know for certain we'll ever have. The wise of us keep this in the forefront of our mind and live each day accordingly, always striving to create good times, and making sure to savor those that we have. Death reminds us to never squander any moment, to relish each and every pleasure, and to be grateful for whatever good life grants us.

(5) Revel in the miniature. Of course, we all want to enjoy those big things in life – a loving, lasting relationship, a vibrant, engaging career, financial security. When we have these, we would be wise to be grateful for them. But we can also take pleasure in and be grateful for the little things as well – the beauty of the snow in the woods behind the house, our child's laughter, the warmth of the blankets in which we snuggle as we go to sleep at night. Such moments are available many times each day. All it takes is for us to be alert to them and to savor them as they present themselves.

Behavioral Strategies

1. Give Yourself Daily Pleasure

"My life is so boring," a thirty-something lawyer recently told me. "All there is in my life is work and TV," a mildly depressed forty-year-old housewife complained. "I've lost the zest for life that I used to have," a fifty-something middle manager shared with me.

With these three people, as I do with all the other patients who voice similar concerns, I took out my mental microscope and checked for an underlying depression. Sometimes I found it, sometimes I didn't. When I did, of course, I tried my best to help the person fix it. But, whether depressed or not, the time always comes when I feel compelled to ask the patient: "What are you going to do to bring more spice into your life?"

You'd think that would open the door to an eager effort to brainstorm, to create a list of pleasurable activities, followed by enthusiastic, determined actions to bring these pleasures into one's life. Some do. But you might be surprised how many people resist swinging into action. They throw up any number of negative reasons to block themselves, to wit:

- It won't make a difference, so why bother?
- I'll have to first feel better emotionally, then we'll see.
- I shouldn't have to work so hard to be happy.
- I just have too much to do.
- What's the point? Life sucks anyway.

These few excuses only scratch the surface. Those who voice these would be wise to realize and embrace the following points which, taken together, provide the best reasons I know for every one of us to purposely build pleasure into our daily lives.

- This is the one and only life we know for sure we will ever have. To waste it with laziness, lethargy, and lassitude is foolish.
- Aristotle, the great American psychologist Albert Ellis, and the Dalai Lama all said it: being happy is what life is all about. To build pleasure into our lives enhances our happiness. To fail to act can easily block our chances for happiness, thereby thwarting that innate purpose of life we all share. How sad.
- You are a human being. No matter what your circumstances are, you have a right – hell, even a responsibility – to bring pleasure and happiness into

your life. There is no psychological, philosophical, or spiritual reason whatsoever by which you should be denied the birthright we all share – pleasure and happiness.

- No one is put on this earth to pleasure you. It's your responsibility to bring happiness into your own life. You want to therefore step up to the plate and do whatever it takes within the boundaries of ethics, morals, and the law to make that happen.
- The bottom line is that the Happiness Fairy will not come knocking on your door to deliver happiness to you. You must act, then act again, and then act some more to populate your life with the daily pleasures you want and deserve.

Here, then, is a five-step plan to give yourself daily pleasure, starting from the inside and moving outward.

(1) Adopt the Right Attitude. Reread, digest, and embrace the five points I articulated above. They can serve as the five pillars to stimulate you to act to make pleasure and happiness a daily guest in your house.

(2) Eliminate Emotional Contamination. If you are suffering from any debilitating emotional problem – persistent anxiety, depression, guilt, or anger – do something to rid yourself of them. I suggest you consult with a competent cognitive – behavior therapist, particularly one who practices Rational Emotive Behavioral Therapy, who can help you rid yourself of this contamination, thereby freeing you to avail yourself of the opportunities for pleasure and happiness in your life.

(3) Brainstorm Pleasurable Experiences. Either alone or with a trusted friend, brainstorm as many pleasurable activities you can that will build pleasure into your daily life. I'm not thinking of biggies like a week in the Caribbean or attending your favorite rock artist's next concert, although I encourage you to go for these larger pleasures whenever you can. What I'm thinking about are those little pleasures that are available to you every day. They might be a bubble bath, lunch with your best friend, a phone call to a loved one, going window shopping, enjoying a TV movie, an hour of pleasurable reading, a nap, a walk in the woods, luxuriating in the hot tub, a massage, and so on and so forth. Go ahead right now: Think of what has and does pleasure you. Make that list.

(4) Get a Support System. Ask a trusted friend to support you in doing in at least one pleasurable thing from your list each day. Have this person to remind

you, encourage you, even badger you if necessary to swing into action. Even better, invite this person to share some of these pleasurable activities with you.

(5) Act, Act, Act. You will experience no pleasure unless you act. Imagine your house getting painted simply by you thinking about painting it, planning to paint it, talking about painting it. The only way to get it painted is to paint it. So, engage in these pleasurable activities; one a day keeps the doctor away.

2. Rid Unnecessary Negatives

As you know, we do not live in the best of all possible worlds. There are wars and terrorists. There is bigotry in all its ugly forms. There are hurricanes and plane crashes and child abuse. There are also all the annoying minor things that seem to pop up to devil us – the flu, the washing machine that breaks down, the traffic congestion we have to endure to get to and from work.

So many of the negatives we face in life – large and small – are largely beyond our control. There is little we can do to prevent or eliminate them. Our challenge, then, is to lump them as gracefully as we can.

But, guess what? Many of these negatives we can control. We don't have to wait till they happen and then react. We can do something about them, if only we are willing to take the time and make the effort to do so. We can indeed follow Reinhold Niebuhr's Serenity Prayer: "God grant me the courage to change the things I can, the serenity to accept the things I can't, and the wisdom to know the difference."

In this vein, what follows are three steps to rid those unnecessary annoyances that pollute your life. Go for it.

(1) Take the right attitude. The bottom line is that your time on earth is limited. There may be an afterlife, but we don't know for sure. This may very well be it. After that, there may be no more. Secondly, it's up to you. Nobody is put on this earth to make your life work. It's your job. Your happiness is your responsibility. This includes both bringing pleasure into your life and eliminating as much of the pain and negative as is humanly possible. Finally, you have to get off your butt. Nothing changes without doing what's necessary to make the change happen. You must swing into action and systematically – relentlessly, day after day – act to clean out the unnecessary negatives from your life. You deserve to do so. You are entitled to do so. You can do so, if you willingly swing into action.

(2) Do an inventory. With pencil and paper, draw a line down the middle. Then, on the left side, list those things in your life that you find frustrating and annoying including those people who bring negativity to your life. Don't censor yourself. Be complete. Then, on the right half of the page, decide what to do to either rid yourself of that annoyance or modify it some way to make it less onerous. But remember, with regard to the people, putting them on this list doesn't qualify them as bad or worthless, only frustrating to you.

(3) Use the Serenity Prayer to game plan. Now reflect on your two lists. Decide which of these you can eliminate without bringing undue harm to yourself or to others? Which do you have to gracefully tolerate as one of those unavoidable thorns in your life?

(4) For those negative events you can't get rid of, work hard to keep them in perspective so as to not cause yourself unnecessary misery.

(5) Act. For those you can rid, select one item each month and eliminate it from your life. Start by picking one for this month. What is it? What can you do to eliminate it from your life? Can you simply get rid of it? Can you get someone else to handle it for you? Can you alter it in some way so that it is no longer troublesome? Figure out what to do, and then follow through – immediately. Then next month, eliminate another one, then another the month after, and on and on. Continue this for the next twelve months. Just think how different your life will look a year from now.

3. Practice Breakthrough, Not Breakdown

There is a story about Albert Einstein that bears repeating. When someone once asked him what he thought was the most important question any human being needed to answer, he responded, "Is the universe friendly or not?"

For sure, how you answer this question will drive you toward either happiness or unhappiness. If you think the universe to be friendly, then you will likely be grateful for the past, attentive to the good in the present, and be hopeful about the future. If, on the other hand, you think the universe to be unfriendly, then you will likely focus on the negatives, whine about the struggles, and hold a pessimistic view of the future.

But I'm not sure Einstein posed the right question. The truth of the matter is that the world is neither friendly nor unfriendly. It just is, as it is, at the moment it is, with all the friendly and unfriendly circumstances in it at that time. In fact, the universe is impersonal. If you think about it, the universe as such doesn't even know you exist.

I suggest, therefore, that there is a better question to ask: "How will I react when I face life's unfriendly circumstances?" If you start with the premise that there will be hardships in everyone's life, including yours – sometimes hassles and annoyances, other times calamities and even tragedies – then there are two ways you can react when you face misfortune:

One way to act is with Breakdown Thinking. You perceive yourself to be a victim of the unwanted circumstances. That is, you hold the universe responsible for your happiness. So, when faced with unwanted circumstances, you resort to protesting ("This shouldn't be!"), whining ("Why me?"), and/or blaming ("Damn you!" "Damn me!" "Damn it!"), instead of going about the business of doing what can be done to improve the situation.

The unfortunate consequences of this mentality are many. One is that you now have to contend with two adversities for the price of one: The adversity and the emotional contamination of depression, self-pity, and bitterness that this type of thinking spawns. Two, you are unlikely to take action to improve the adverse situation itself, so that you are faced with dealing with it indefinitely. A third is that the breakdown mentality tends to get more deeply habituated in you, so that, when the next unfriendly circumstance occurs, you will more likely respond in these unhappy, nonproductive ways than before.

The second is Breakthrough Thinking. With this mentality, you take responsibility for your own life, as per, "How I respond to this adversity is up to me." When an adversity erupts, instead of protesting, whining, or blaming, you go into problem solving mode and do your best to make the situation as good as you can. Instead of asking, "Why me?" you ask the following questions:

• What is the opportunity in this breakdown for a breakthrough?
• What is my best next move?
• What can I learn from this experience that could serve me well in the future?

Notice how these questions focus you away from victimhood and emotional misery and toward constructive action. The truth is, most situations can be improved upon, if not totally resolved. Furthermore, even if you cannot immediately resolve the unfriendly situation, you need not make oneself miserable about it by protesting, whining, and/or blaming.

Here are a few ideas you can use to help yourself to think and act in a breakthrough manner when you face the inevitable vicissitudes of life.

(1) Make an Attitude Inventory. Review the last ten adversities you faced. What was your automatic way of thinking? Was it Breakdown or Breakthrough? Whether Breakdown or Breakthrough, what was the emotional experience you had that went with it? Did it help or hinder you to engage in problem solving?

(2) Commit to the Breakthrough Attitude. Make a conscious choice to respond to future adversities by using the breakthrough questions I posted above.

(3) Do a Life Inventory. Find a quiet time to reflect on your life. Look to the past. Is there anything you feel bitter, guilty, or depressed about? If so, apply the breakthrough mentality to it with an eye to doing something that will provide a breakthrough. Do the same for your present life. Also, scan the future to see if there is anything you anticipate that may happen that you can proactively handle in a breakthrough way. In other words, go about the business of cleaning up your life, without resorting to the victim's toolbox: Protesting, whining, and/or blaming.

Your Happiness with Life Action Plan

As with Chapters 4, 5, and 6, now is your opportunity to start thinking about how you might use the ideas and strategies in this chapter so as to increase your happiness with life quotient. Please review the preceding pages and see what you might want to start doing immediately and also what you might want to include in your first Happiness Action Plan you will create in Chapter 9.

Prompt One: Practicing Perspective. Identify three situations about which you tend to bring unhappiness upon yourself through catastrophizing. For each, create a perspective that can help you gracefully lump these adversities.

	Adversity	New Perspective
1.	_____	_____
	_____	_____
	_____	_____
2.	_____	_____
	_____	_____
	_____	_____

3. _____   _____

   _____   _____

   _____   _____

Prompt Two: Additional Happiness with Life Strategies. Select two additional perspective strategies that you think would help you feel more happy with life. Determine exactly what you will do to implement them and where and when you will do it.

	Strategy	What	Where/When
1.	_____	_____	_____
	_____	_____	_____
2.	_____	_____	_____
	_____	_____	_____
3.	_____	_____	_____
	_____	_____	_____

Going Forward

This chapter has been all about finding happiness in your daily life. It started with the breakthrough strategy of Perspective. Following that, I described six powerful strategies to enhance your happiness quotient. I now look forward to joining you in Chapter 8: "Live Your Ethical Principles."

Notes

8

LIVE YOUR ETHICAL PRINCIPLES

Imagine attending one of my personal empowerment seminars. Along with twenty or so of your peers, you sit around the outside of rectangular tables arranged into the shape of a giant horseshoe. Standing at the open end, I announce that we're going to start with a group exercise. With that, I instruct all of you to "Close your eyes and keep them closed until I tell you to open them."

Most of you immediately comply, but a few shoot me a nervous look. "Don't worry," I say, "I promise I won't embarrass anyone." Then, when everyone has their eyes closed, I add, "Now, without poking anyone, point to the north, but, whatever you do, don't peek until I tell you to look."

I watch in amusement as fingers point in every conceivable direction – left and right, backward and forward, some even upward. I then tell all of you to keep pointing, then to open your eyes and look around. Inevitably, peals of laughter ring out.

Once the laughter subsides, I ask, "Is it important to know what direction is north?" Most of you nod affirmatively and cite such examples as when hiking in the wilderness, navigating a boat in open water, or piloting an aircraft.

This then leads to my second question: "If we needed to locate north, how would we do it?" Your answers range from the primitive, for example, the stars, sunrise and sunset, and moss on a tree, to the more scientific, a compass or a sextant.

Then I deliver the punch line. "Just as true north, using whatever method we need to locate it, enables us to determine and stay on our physical bearing, so too do the core principles upon which we stand guide us in all our personal decisions and actions."

I explain what I mean by the example of the seemingly irreconcilable conflicts that now plague the U.S. federal government in Washington, DC. For the Republicans, the bedrock principles are individual liberty and the rule of law.

With apologies for the pun, these two principles trump all others. In contrast, the Democrats hold compassion as their highest principle. For them, if there is a conflict between compassion and the law, they opt for compassion. With such disparate principles driving their thinking, it is little wonder the two parties bitterly fight over such issues as immigration, federal mandated health care, taxes, federal judgeships, and entitlements. What is proper and honorable to one party is abhorrent and loathsome to the other.

This then leads me to assert five truths about the power of principles in order to lead a happy life.

1. Our principles are our personal code of right conduct. They form the basis of what we might call our character.
2. We all have principles. They may be good or bad, honorable or dishonorable, self-enhancing or self-defeating. Regardless, we cannot help but develop them through our life experiences.
3. The principles we hold greatly influence all our decisions and actions. Consider Aristotle's Table of Virtues illustrated in Table 8.1 (1955). He thought virtues, his term for principles, to be the mean between two vices – one an excess of that virtue, the other a deficiency. For example, he asserted that the principle of courage is the mean between the excess of rashness and that of cowardice. The person who adopted the principle of courage would respond to life situations quite differently than a person endorsing either of the extremes.
4. Most of us do not consciously reflect upon, determine, or draw upon our core principles when navigating through our daily lives. As a result, we easily fall into a reactive posture, responding to situations by immediate impulse, emotion, and/or whim. In other words, without a conscious, carefully selected set of principles to guide our decisions and actions, our lives play out at the effect of forces beyond our awareness and intention, leaving our choices and thus our happiness to chance.
5. Consciously determining, remembering, and acting on our true north principles gives us a leg up on taking charge of our lives and bringing ourselves as much satisfaction and happiness as possible. Furthermore, the more we practice them, the more habituated they become.

Having established the primacy of principles in life, let's now put you to work in the Sacred Principles workshop. I encourage you to fully invest your best in this as if your future happiness depends on it, because it does.

Table 8.1 Aristotle's Table of Virtues

Excess	Virtue/Principle	Deficiency
Rashness	Courage	Cowardice
Self-Indulgence	Temperance	Insensibility
Prodigality	Liberality	Meanness
Vulgarity	Magnificence	Pettiness
Vanity	Magnanimity	Pusillanimity
Ambition	Pride	Unambitiousness
Irascibility	Patience	Lack of spirit
Boastfulness	Truthfulness	Mock modesty
Buffoonery	Wittiness	Boorishness
Obsequiousness	Friendliness	Cantankerousness
Shyness	Modesty	Shamelessness
Envy	Righteous indignation	Maliciousness/spiteful

Breakthrough Strategy Five: Your Sacred Principles

Think of the Passionate Purpose you created in Chapter 4 to be the *why* of your life – the reason behind what you do on a day-to-day basis. Your Sacred Principles, then, tells you *how* to act in the process of fulfilling your Purpose.

As with your Passionate Purpose Workshop, determining your principles constitutes three-steps: (1) reflecting on your principles; (2) creating your Principles; and (3) living them throughout the fabric of your life. As you work through these steps, I urge you to be true to yourself, because what you produce in this workshop will be your personal code of right conduct, a key ingredient to living a happy life.

Step One: Reflection

Before you craft your Sacred Principles, please reflect upon the following questions. They can provide the insights to help you create the core principles that you would be proud to follow as you conduct your life.

1. Name three people whom you most admire and respect. What qualities do they possess that leads you to hold them in such high esteem?

    For me, they are my father, my college basketball coach, Arad McCutchan, and my clinical psychology mentor, Dr. Albert Ellis. As much or more than anyone else I've ever known, my father embodied the ability to be emotionally open, caring, and compassionate, without fear of judgment or embarrassment. Arad McCutchan possessed a miraculous combination of focused competitiveness and a perspective that allowed him to never take himself or life too seriously. And Dr. Ellis demonstrated the power of critical thinking and reasoning to such a degree that he revolutionized the field of psychotherapy. As you will soon see, I borrowed liberally from each of these role models in formulating my own Sacred Principles.

- **Person 1:**
  Most Admired Qualities:

  _____

  _____

  _____

- **Person 2:**
  Most Admired Qualities:

  _____

  _____

  _____

- **Person 3:**
  Most Admired Qualities:

  _____

  _____

  _____

2. In what ways do you most value being treated by others? What is the profound benefit you get from being the recipient of these?

   I value, among other things, being treated with respect, being taken seriously, and being listened to when I have something I want to share. I also value affection, affirmation, and appreciation. Furthermore, I value intellectually stimulating conversations mixed with humor, goodwill, and a mutual search for the truth.

   I could go on, but I think you get the picture. List below up to five ways in which you desire to be treated by others. For each, articulate why it is important to you.

- **Value 1:**
  Why Important:

  _____

  _____

  _____

- **Value 2:**
  Why Important:

  _____

  _____

  _____

- **Value 3:**
  Why Important:

  _____

  _____

  _____

- **Value 4:**
  Why Important:

  _____

  _____

  _____

- **Value 5:**
  Why Important:

  _____

  _____

  _____

3. Among the way you act, which do you most value? What positive contributions do you want these actions to make to yourself, to others and/or to the world at large?

   I doubt that I am any different from you, but I value acting proactively to reach my goals and fulfill my Passionate Purpose. I value keeping things in perspective, so as not to overreact emotionally, acting boldly without fear of failure, and staying fit and vibrant. I value acting lovingly and kindly to others, most importantly to my friends and loved ones.

Now, what about you? How would you ideally like to act with regard to yourself, others, and your life in general?

With regard to yourself?

_____

_____

_____

With regard to others?

_____

_____

_____

With regard to your life in general?

_____

_____

_____

Step Two: Create Your Sacred Principles

Excellent job on this first Step. Now it's time for you to create the first draft of your own set of Sacred Principles. You've already seen Aristotle's. By way of illustration, I will also share my own, preceded by my Passionate Purpose, as they ideally go together as a set. Remember that I offer mine only as an example. Please feel free to create principles that truly reflect your own values.

My Passionate Purpose

To make my life, the lives of my loved ones, and the lives of those with whom I relate and work perfect, as they want it. To do this, I will be consistently excellent in living, modeling, and teaching the strategies for effective and joyful living.

My Sacred Principles

As I fulfill my purpose, I commit to these principles to guide all my decisions and behaviors:

- Personal Responsibility. I will take full responsibility for all my thoughts, actions, and feelings, never being a victim or whining about what I don't like. I will keep all my commitments and promises, regardless of time and circumstances, and I will view all breakdowns as opportunities for breakthroughs.
- Loving and Giving. I will be relentlessly loving and giving to others. I will be empathic, compassionate, generous, supportive, and accepting, never winning at their expense. I will do so even when they fail to act as I would want them to do.
- Self-Accepting. I will be thoroughly and totally self-accepting. I will not expect myself to be perfect, understand that I am a valid human being, even with all my flaws and mistakes, and know that I do not have to prove my worth to myself or anyone else.
- Perspective. I will accept that life will be difficult at times and that others will act fallibly and imperfectly, thereby challenging me with hardships, hassles, and frustrations. I will not whine or catastrophize about them, demand that they not be so, or damn any person or situation. I will keep a sense of humor, all the while viewing difficulties as an opportunity to learn, grow, and break through.
- Balance and Renewal. I will balance immediate pleasure with sound preparation for the future. To do so, I will: Combine a healthy mind with a healthy body, by eating correctly, exercising regularly, and resting sufficiently; balancing work with pleasure in order to remain sharp and refreshed; and spending regular time challenging myself intellectually and expanding my knowledge base.

Now, dear reader, it's your turn. Drawing from your reflections in Step One, write the first draft of the Sacred Principles you will commit to follow every day as you act out your Passionate Purpose. Remember that there are no right or wrong principles, so long as they are true to you and are within ethical, moral, and legal bounds.

1. _____

_____

_____

2. _____

_____

_____

3. _____

_____

_____

4. _____

_____

_____

5. _____

_____

_____

Step Three: Live It

All the best intentions in the world will be for naught unless translated into action. Accordingly, I personally review each morning my Passionate Purpose and my Sacred Principles. Then I look through my day's schedule to see the opportunities I have to live my Purpose in a principled way. Then all I have to do is follow through that day, one day at a time.

What about you? When, where, and how will you find it most valuable to consciously and purposely live your Sacred Principles? Be as thorough and explicit as possible.

	Principle	Where/When	With Whom	How
•	_____	_____	_____	_____
	_____	_____	_____	_____
•	_____	_____	_____	_____
	_____	_____	_____	_____
•	_____	_____	_____	_____
	_____	_____	_____	_____

- _____ _____ _____ _____
  _____ _____ _____ _____
- _____ _____ _____ _____
  _____ _____ _____ _____

Additional Sacred Principles Strategies

A music teacher who attended one of my workshops once remarked, "If I don't get up each morning and set the tone, other people and events will." Your Sacred Principles, along with your Passionate Purpose, provides you an opportunity to do just that. With this one and only life you know for sure you'll ever have, it would be foolish not to do so.

What I now share with you are five strategies that can help you make the most of your principles throughout the fabric of your daily life. Remember that nothing changes unless you act, so these strategies provide an opportunity to translate good sentiment into results-driven action. See which ones you might find profitable to help you live out your Sacred Principles going forward.

1. Think and Act Proactively

Like me, start off each morning with a review of what you will face that day. Make explicit how you might use the day's challenges to express your Passionate Purpose and act according to your Sacred Principles. By doing this, you will be surprised to discover how many opportunities you will find to bring meaning and fulfillment to each of your days. This strategy will also provide you with the best chance of producing your intended results, thereby bringing about even more pleasure and satisfaction.

2. Call Time Out and Reflect

It is so easy to get caught up in the hurly-burly of everyday life. There are those never-ending chores, the unexpected demands at both work and home, the crises that inevitably arise, and on and on. Given all this, there is the probability that you will, without using your compass to guide you, fall into a reactive posture, reflexively responding to the latest challenges despite your principles, thereby threatening your well-being and peace of mind.

Take pains to be alert to these moments and take a few moments to reground yourself. Ask yourself: What's the problem with which I'm now dealing? Does my Passionate Purpose give me guidance as to how to respond? Which of my principles do I need to follow as I address this situation? What's my best next move? Armed with the answers to these questions, then act boldly.

3. Debrief at Night

Each night before bedtime review your day. With regard to accomplishing your goals, acting out your Passionate Purpose, and living your Sacred Principles, reflect on what you can learn for tomorrow about producing your cherished results and finding personal satisfaction. Ask yourself: What did I do well that I want to continue? What did I do marginally well that I could improve upon? What mistakes did I make that I can correct? What did I not do that would be helpful to start doing?

As you conduct this debriefing, be careful to not berate yourself, others, or life circumstances. Don't lose sight of the fact that this exercise is an opportunity for improvement, not for blaming and whining. Onward and upward.

4. Join a Band

Tom Petty is one of my all-time favorite rockers. I have relished his music all the way from when I heard his first CD, *Tom Petty and the Heartbreakers*, through the concert I attended in Baltimore, Maryland a few weeks before his death.

In addition to being a creative genius, Petty was also famous for relishing being in a band. First there was the Epics, when he was a gangly teenager, then came Mudcrutch in his late teens and early adulthood, and lastly the Heartbreakers. But he didn't want to be in just any old band, one like the Beach Boys, which carried its name forward, but completely changed its musicians. Rather, he wanted to grow and develop as an artist with the same group of people over a lifetime. And he mostly pulled that off, dying in the company of the same people that he made music with most of his career.

In the spirit of Tom Petty and the Heartbreakers, you too would benefit from belonging to a supporting group of people with whom you too can rock. This group of people, committed to supporting you and each other in living your Sacred Principles, can serve as a consciousness-raiser, a safe place for constructive feedback and accountability, and a source of reinforcement for positive action.

5. Teach, Teach, Teach

It is a well-known fact that we deepen our understanding of something when we teach it to others. That is one of the unexpected benefits I've drawn from practicing psychotherapy. I have the opportunity to personally engrain and deepen what I teach my patients each and every hour. Opportunities too abound for you to do just that in the context of your own life – with your significant other, your children, your colleagues at work. The list goes on. All of these people provide an opportunity for you, as an individual, to keep your own personal principles front and center in your mind, so that you can reap the benefits.

Your Sacred Principles Happiness Action Plan

As you did in Chapter 4 with regard to your Passionate Purpose, take some time to review the contents of this chapter, then record below a second draft of your Sacred Principles. After that, list what you will do to express it through the significant roles in your life. Finally, note two additional strategies you could use to help you act according to these principles.

My Sacred Principles

1. _____

    _____

    _____

2. _____

    _____

    _____

3. _____

    _____

    _____

4. _____

    _____

    _____

5. _____

_____

_____

My Roles

My Roles	Where, When, With Whom
1.	
2.	
3.	
4.	
5.	

Additional Strategies

Strategies	Where, When, With Whom
1.	
2.	
3.	

4.   _____   _____

     _____   _____

5.   _____   _____

     _____   _____

Going Forward

In this chapter, I've tried to emphasize the importance of consciously defining and purposely living your Sacred Principles to your ongoing happiness and well-being. I also offered you five additional strategies to help you keep your principles alive and vibrant throughout each day of your life.

Before you move on to Chapter 9, in which you will craft your own personalized, comprehensive Happiness Action Plan, I invite you to take a bit of time to review what you've learned in this chapter that you have found useful.

Notes

PART III

YOUR HAPPINESS ACTION PLAN

Most of us take pains to organize the responsibilities and events that populate our lives. We jot down the groceries to buy before heading to the store, the Christmas list before fighting the crowds at the mall, the stops we need to make around town as we take care of one piece of business after another. We note on the family calendar our next dentist appointment, the trip to the hairstylist, the kids' soccer games. We detail what needs to be done before the New Year's Eve party, our daughter's college graduation reception, that European vacation.

Yet, how many of us take the time to plan the arc of the successful career we want, the loving marriage we desire, the happy life we long for? Not many, I think you'll agree.

So, here in Part III: Your Happiness Action Plan is your chance to do just that. Notice that I said "do." If you determine exactly what you need to do, and then relentlessly go about doing it, you will have the best chance of securing the life you love to live.

In Part III, then, you are to create the action plan that will give you the happiness you want and deserve. As you do so, please heed the following five guidelines. They can help you devise a realistic plan that will be both workable and productive.

1. Be Confident

Yes, you can bring happiness into your life. You've seen the multitude of strategies to do so throughout this book – both mental and behavioral. They've worked for countless others, and they can also work for you. All you have to do is follow through on those you choose.

2. Start Moderately

Don't make the mistake of crowding your Happiness Action Plan with so many strategies that you overwhelm yourself. Remember that you do have a normal life to lead with all of its responsibilities and chores. Start your HAP with what's manageable. You don't have to use strategies from every chapter. You don't have to immediately act on every one you find valuable. Pick and choose what will work for you. You can always add more strategies later on as you experience successes.

3. Be Realistic

In crafting your Happiness Action Plan, don't expect an overwhelming wave of happiness to immediately wash over you all at once. Start with building fun and pleasure into your daily life, not total happiness, much less the rare experience of joy. As you experience more fun and pleasure, the more likely you will be to look back on your day and judge that it was a happy one.

4. Take the Experimental Approach

If there's some strategy on your Happiness Action Plan that doesn't produce the pleasurable results you want, try something else. Rigidity and stubbornness are your enemies, while flexibility and adaptability are your allies. Heed the old adage, "If at first you don't succeed, try, try again."

5. Reach Out

As silly as it may sound at first blush, one of the more valuable insights is that what you don't see and appreciate will greatly limit your happiness. When I, for example, don't know something, but I don't know that I don't know it, I blindly continue in my old self-defeating ways, frustrated that I keep getting the same undesirable results. This is exactly where people you trust, your teammates so to speak, can help you spot what you may have missed. They can help hone your Happiness Action Plan to be the best it can be. So, put silly pride aside and reach out to others for input.

With these guidelines in mind, now tackle Chapter 9: "Creating Your Happiness Action Plan." Remember that you have every right to be happy. Go for it. Hold nothing back.

9

CREATING YOUR HAPPINESS
ACTION PLAN

As you create your Happiness Action Plan, take whatever time you find necessary, whether that be a single sitting or several sittings spread over many days. Remember that this is your plan, not anyone else's, so make it real, genuine, and useful to you. Above all, remember that you are worth whatever time and effort it takes to get it right.

In each of the following five steps, select the exact strategies from Part II: The Happiness Practices you think will help you build more and more happiness into your life. Only include those strategies that you think would be of benefit. And don't forget you can always modify your plan later as you wish.

My Happiness Action Plan

Step One: Happiness Through My Purpose and Principles

Remember that true happiness transcends momentary pleasure. It comes about in large measure by acting over time both in the service of your Passionate Purpose and in accordance with your Sacred Principles. Accordingly, start this first step of your Happiness Action Plan by thoughtfully reviewing both the passionate purpose you created in Chapter 4: "Live Your Passionate Purpose" and the sacred principles you crafted in Chapter 8: "Live Your Sacred Principles." Then, finalize both of them below. Following that, brainstorm how you will actually integrate them through the significant roles you play in your life. Finally, note what additional strategies from Chapters 4 and 8 you think might help you find happiness through your Purpose and Principles.

My Passionate Purpose

_____

_____

_____

_____

_____

_____

_____

_____

_____

_____

_____

_____

_____

_____

My Sacred Principles

As I act out my Passionate Purpose, I will do so according to these Sacred Principles:

- _____

  _____

  _____

- _____

  _____

  _____

- _____

  _____

  _____

- _____

  _____

  _____

- _____
  _____
  _____

Living My Purpose and Principles

Role	Where/When/With Whom	Expression

- _____   _____   _____
  _____   _____   _____

- _____   _____   _____
  _____   _____   _____

- _____   _____   _____
  _____   _____   _____

- _____   _____   _____
  _____   _____   _____

- _____   _____   _____
  _____   _____   _____

Additional Purpose and Principle Strategies

Strategy	How Experienced

- _____   _____
  _____   _____

- _____   _____
  _____   _____

- _____   _____
  _____   _____

- _____   _____
  _____   _____

- _____   _____
  _____   _____

Step Two: Happiness with Yourself

Start this step by carefully reviewing the contents of Chapter 5: "Happiness With Yourself." Pay special attention to the Breakthrough Strategy of Unconditional Self-Acceptance. By unconditionally accepting yourself, you can live free of the misery of anxiety, depression, guilt, and shame. Don't forget to also look over the six additional self-happiness strategies I described to strengthen your ability to be happy with yourself, as well as any notes you may have made at the end of the chapter.

Once you've refreshed your memory, determine first what practices you think will help you unconditionally accept yourself. For each, note exactly what you will do and where and when you will do it. Then, make note of any additional strategies you think could help you to increase your happiness quotient with yourself. As before, determine exactly what you will do and where and when you will do it.

Unconditional Self-Acceptance Strategies

Strategy	What	Where/When
• _____	_____	_____
_____	_____	_____
• _____	_____	_____
_____	_____	_____
• _____	_____	_____
_____	_____	_____
• _____	_____	_____
_____	_____	_____
• _____	_____	_____
_____	_____	_____

Additional Happiness with Self Strategies

Strategy	What	Where/When
• _____	_____	_____
_____	_____	_____
• _____	_____	_____
_____	_____	_____
• _____	_____	_____
_____	_____	_____
• _____	_____	_____
_____	_____	_____
• _____	_____	_____
_____	_____	_____

Step Three: Happiness with Others

As you may recall, being happy with the people in your life requires you to hold realistic expectations about them. While they can indeed provide you with some of your greatest joys, they will also deliver some of your greatest disappointments and frustrations. After all, you live among flawed, fallible people, not saints or angels. Confronted with this reality, you have two choices. One is to become bitter and angry, thereby destroying your happiness. The second is to adopt the breakthrough strategy of Premeditated Acceptance and Forgiveness, a perspective that helps you to be realistic in your expectations of others, take nothing they do personal, and relate with them without bitterness, hurt, and anger.

Start this step by thoughtfully reviewing the contents of Chapter 6: "Happiness with Others." Be sure to especially digest the ins and outs of the breakthrough strategy of Premeditated Acceptance and Forgiveness, then refamiliarize yourself with the additional cognitive and behavioral strategies I shared and the notes you made at the end of the chapter. Once you absorb all this, list the cognitive and behavioral strategies you think would help you practice Premeditated Acceptance and Forgiveness. For each, note with whom you will consciously apply them. Then, to complete Step Three, select what additional strategies you will employ to help you find pleasure and happiness in your life. Remember that your happiness is at stake. Devote quality time and thought to selecting and refining these strategies.

Premeditated Acceptance and Forgiveness Strategies

Strategy with Whom	Where/When
• _____	_____
_____	_____
• _____	_____
_____	_____
• _____	_____
_____	_____
• _____	_____
_____	_____
• _____	_____
_____	_____

Additional Happiness with Others Strategies

Strategy	Where/When
• _____	_____
_____	_____
• _____	_____
_____	_____
• _____	_____
_____	_____

- _____   _____
  _____   _____
- _____   _____
  _____   _____

Happiness with Life

The theme of Chapter 7, "Being Happy with Life," is that, while life does indeed deliver to all of us our fair share of hardships and hassles, we need not be miserable about them. By adopting the breakthrough strategy of Perspective, we can learn to gracefully lump these frustrations without succumbing to misery. This then opens the door to consciously bringing pleasure into each of our days.

In preparation for the work to follow, take whatever time you need to reacquaint yourself with the contents of Chapter 7. After you have done this prep work, first brainstorm how and about what it would benefit you to practice Perspective. Then, from the additional happiness with life strategies I shared in that chapter, list all those you think might bring more happiness to your life.

Additional Happiness with Life Strategies

	Strategy	With Whom	Where/When
•	_____	_____	_____
	_____	_____	_____
•	_____	_____	_____
	_____	_____	_____
•	_____	_____	_____
	_____	_____	_____
•	_____	_____	_____
	_____	_____	_____
•	_____	_____	_____
	_____	_____	_____

Step Five: Review and Finalize

In the spirit of Goldilocks and the Three Bears, you want your Happiness Action Plan to be neither too big nor too small, too hard nor too soft, too hot nor too cool. You want it to be just right. So now is the time to take a final look at what you've created. Ask yourself: Have I included too much or too little? Have I emphasized one element at the expense of another? Have I overlooked something important in my quest for happiness? With these questions in your mind, carefully go back over your HAP and revise it as needed.

Going Forward

Excellent. Now you have it – your own, comprehensive action plan to bring you pleasure, satisfaction, and, yes, happiness into your life. Who knows, you may even surprise yourself by even experiencing occasional moments of out-and-out joy.

Remember that you are worth the effort. But, also remember that happiness won't come seeking you out. If it's going to be, you'll have to make it happen. If you act on your plan – day after day – you have a good chance of increasing your happiness. So, get off your derriere, get to work, now, today, and make it happen. You will want to:

- Review it each morning to keep it forefront in your mind as you travel through your day;
- Take a few minutes in the evening to debrief how well you did that day so you can make important corrections the next;
- Make adjustments as needed.

When you're ready, move ahead to Chapters 10 and 11, where I provide you with tools from the worlds of both psychology and philosophy that can aid you to follow through to success. See you there.

Notes

PART IV

SUSTAINING HAPPINESS FOR LIFE

Throughout this book I have emphasized that the only way to bring about lasting happiness is to do what is necessary to make it happen – purposely and relentlessly. To nail that point, let me describe a simple demonstration I often conduct in my personal empowerment workshops.

To start the demonstration, I recruit a volunteer from the audience. With a pencil laying in my open palm, I say to her, "Now, *try* to take the pencil from my hand."

Inevitably, she looks quizzically at me, then abruptly grabs the pencil away as if I'm going to pull some devious trick at the last second. One volunteer did this so forcefully that she drew blood scratching my hand with her fingernails.

Typically, the audience laughs, me included. Once quieted, I ask the group, "Did she follow my instructions?"

Most everybody responds in the affirmative.

"Are you sure?" I ask. "Did she in fact follow my instructions to *try* to take the pencil from my hand?"

Most often some astute members of the audience get it. They pipe up and say: "No, she didn't follow your instructions. You told her to try to take the pencil, not take it."

"Ahh," I say, "so there's a big difference between trying to take the pencil and actually taking it, isn't there?" Then I turn back to the volunteer and this time make my instructions more explicit: "Now, *try* to take a pencil from my hand, but don't take it – just *try*."

At first gingerly, then in more animated ways, she grimaces and strains, circling my hand from various angles, her fingers claw-like and her forearm taut, but never quite taking the pencil from my hand. While she's doing this, I encourage the audience to chant, "Try! Try! Try!"

After a few seconds of this, I call her trying to a halt and ask everybody, "So, what's the results she got from trying?" Without waiting for an answer, I emphatically exclaim: "Nothing! No result is ever produced by trying. You only get a result by doing."

To conclude the demonstration, I again place the pencil in my open palm and give the volunteer a radically different instruction: "Now, don't just try, actually take the pencil from my hand." When she does, I melodramatically raise my hands above head in triumph and say, "Ta-daaa."

Then I conclude the demonstration by sharing with the audience what I call *The Two Rules for Producing Extraordinary Performance and Results:*

Rule 1: The only thing that will produce an intended result is to do exactly what is necessary to produce that result. Trying won't do it. Hoping won't. Neither will praying. Only by doing what's necessary will produce that result.

Rule 2: You, and only you, are responsible for producing the results you want in your life. To produce them, you must take responsibility to do whatever is necessary, whatever that be, within, of course, moral, ethical, and legal bounds.

What follows in the next two chapters, then, are strategies you can adopt to help you do what is necessary to act on your Happiness Action Plan. Chapter 10 focuses on psychological strategies and Chapter 11 draws on the world of philosophy. Please carefully read them and adopt whatever strategies you find useful. Remember: If it's going to be, it's up to you.

10

SUSTAINING HAPPINESS ACTION

The Psychological Way

In his seminal book, *Talent Is Overrated* (2008), Geoff Colvin proves that Thomas Jefferson got it right. He provides a wealth of information from a wide swath of fields that showed that it is hard, sustained work, not talent, that distinguishes high achievers from their more average brethren. This proved to be true from the world of business through that of athletics and even into the arts.

Malcolm Gladwell goes one step further. In his book *Outliers: The Story of Success* (2008, p. 40), he tells us that it is the consensus among experts that ten thousand hours of practice are needed for a person to truly reach a level of mastery. In support of this, he quoted the noted neurologist, Daniel Levitin, who wrote:

> The emerging picture from such studies is that ten thousand hours of practice is required to achieve the level of mastery associated with being a world-class expert – in anything. In study after study of composers, basketball players, fiction writers, ice skaters, concert pianists, chess players, master criminals, and what have you, this number comes up again and again. It seems that it takes the brain this long to assimilate all that it needs to know to achieve true mastery.

I can think of no better example of this than the Beatles. They seemingly burst overnight into global superstardom after they first appeared on *The Ed Sullivan* show in 1964. What the world didn't know was that they had already labored in obscurity for a full seven years. During those years, they played live an estimated twelve hundred times, performing anywhere from five to eight consecutive hours at a time. It took a full ten years before the Beatles hit their genius stride with their masterpiece albums, *Rubber Soul, Revolver, Sgt. Pepper's Lonely Hearts Club Band, The Beatles (White Album)*, and *Abbey Road.*

Sounds simple, doesn't it? Just like the Beatles, put in the time, do the work, and reap the benefits. But, there's a hitch. Nobody, but nobody, can sustain the motivation to work so long and hard 100% of the time. No matter how prized the result, a person will be highly motivated to achieve at times, but not so at others. Suffice it to say that, as a by-product of the vagaries of human existence, even for the most cherished outcomes, peoples' enthusiasm for anything will wax and wane.

But, despair not, for this is where the science of psychology comes to the rescue. It provides at least five tried and true strategies to help you sustain the effort you need to reach your goal of happiness. Please consider putting them to use, for they can help you forge ahead when you run across those inevitable wane days.

Five Strategies for Sustaining Action

Strategy One: Leverage Pleasure and Pain

It is a well-established fact that we humans are pleasure seeking and pain avoiding creatures. All things being equal, we naturally act to find pleasure and bypass pain. The rub, though, is that we often let pleasure and pain run us to our detriment rather than purposely leveraging it to our advantage.

This certainly was true for forty-two-year-old Mike, who presented with an addiction to pornography. With desperation in his voice, he told me that he had failed to break this habit with his two prior psychotherapists, both of whom I knew and respected. Worst of all, his wife, who he said he dearly loved, threatened to divorce him if he didn't conquer it this go-around.

Over the course of the next few weeks, I found out why Mike and his two prior therapists had failed. Like with them, he actively engaged in his face-to-face sessions with me, but he neither followed through on the between-session assignments I gave him nor did he make any effort to deny himself pornography.

I knew that I too would fail with him if didn't figure out what drove these self-defeating choices. That's when I pulled out my ace-in-the-hole – leveraging pleasure and pain. Together, we compiled as comprehensive a list as we could of the benefits (pleasures) and costs (pain) to him to his both doing and not doing pornography. You can see what we created in Table 10.1.

Once completed, I then asked Mike two questions. First, when he contemplated visiting the porn site, did he focus on the benefits/pleasures or the costs/pains. In a nanosecond, he said, "The pleasure, of course." Reversing the question, I then asked him whether he focused on the benefits/pleasures or the costs/pains when he thought about denying himself pornography. "The pains," he immediately said.

Table 10.1 Mike's Pleasures/Pain Analysis

Doing Pornography

Benefits/Pleasures	**Costs/Pains**
• Lots of fun	• Loss of wife
• Sexual thrill	• Wasted time
• New sexual ideas	• Sexual frustration
• Motivated for sex	• Have to sneak online
• Something to talk about	• Feel guilty/sleazy

Not Doing Pornography

Benefits/Pleasures	**Costs/Pains**
• Happy wife, happy life	• Frustration
• Freedom from compulsion	• Time to fill
• More time	• Miss it greatly
• Pride in self-control	• Loss of freedom
• Self-confidence	• Resentment

There it was. Mike's pleasure/pain association worked against him. He focused exclusively on the pleasures pornography provided him, all the while ignoring the potential pains. Concurrently, he focused on the pain of not doing pornography, while ignoring the payoffs of abstinence. To say it another way, his pleasure/pain leveraging motivated him to, one, do pornography and, two, to not use any of his therapy strategies to control his pornography behavior. No wonder he failed in all his previous therapy attempts, not to mention to date with me.

All this I explained to Mike. He and I then devised two strategies to leverage pleasure and pain to his sobriety advantage. Both required him to write on one side of a 4" × 6" card the profound pains of indulging in pornography and, on the other, the substantial pleasure of not doing pornography. In the first strategy, he was to reflect six times a day (breakfast, mid-morning, lunch, mid-afternoon, supper, and mid-evening) for five minutes on the respective pleasures of not doing and the pains of doing pornography. The second strategy required him to carry his card with him at all times and pull it out for review whenever he felt the urge to visit a pornography site.

I am happy to report that, at the time I write this, Mike continues to do his daily leveraging. Most importantly, he has thrown himself into his therapy and has now been pornography-free for over four months. I have confidence that his self-control will get stronger and stronger if he continues to gainfully leverage pleasure and pain to his benefit.

As with Mike, you too might find it helpful to leverage pleasure and pain in your quest for happiness. Similar to him, list below all the pleasures or benefits you will get from acting daily on your Happiness Action Plan. Pay attention to the more profound pleasures, being sure to consider both the long-term ones as well as the more immediate ones. Following that, list all the profound pains or costs you will give yourself if you do not act daily on your Happiness Action Plan. Be expansive. Then, like Mike, create a plan to keep yourself focused on these pleasures and pains.

The profound pleasures I will get from acting on my Happiness Action Plan: _____

_____

_____

The profound pains I will get from failing to act on my Happiness Action Plan:

_____

_____

_____

My plan to keep focused on my pleasure and pain: _____

_____

_____

Strategy 2: Harness Rewards and Punishments

I want to introduce the strategy of harnessing rewards and punishments by describing an experiment in which I was the unsuspecting subject. Years ago I taught a seminar at the University of Virginia, titled Systems of Psychotherapy. In it, I required each student to pick one system and write a term paper describing its theoretical underpinnings, methodology, and efficacy. Among the choices were psychoanalysis, gestalt therapy, Adlerian therapy, transactional analysis, and cognitive-behavior therapy.

For six weeks I lectured, led discussions, and answered questions to the best of my ability. After the last class, I settled in my office to grade the students' papers. I plowed through the first four, all the while bemoaning the fact that I still had eleven more to complete before I was finished. "I'll do one more and then reward myself with a snack break," I told myself, picking up the next paper on the pile.

That's when I saw it. Right there in front of me sat a paper titled "Shaping Dr. Grieger with Behavior Modification." What this clever student did was demonstrate the methodology and efficacy of Behavior Therapy by describing an experiment she conducted rather than write a didactic paper. What she did was to divide her experiment into three two-week blocks. In each, she counted the number of times I looked at her. During the first, she sat stone-faced, totally without any expression, simply staring at me whenever I looked at her. In the second two-week block, she smiled and nodded whenever I made eye contact with her. Then, in the third, she returned to giving me the stone-face whenever I glanced her way.

The results proved to be dramatic. The number of times I looked at her nearly tripled in the second block as compared to the first and the third. What she did was condition me to look at her without my even being aware of it. As you can imagine, I gave this young lady an A for her paper.

We call what was done to me Operant Conditioning, a powerful law of learning discovered by the famous American psychologist B. F. Skinner (1974). Operant Conditioning rests on the principle that what follows a behavior has a powerful impact upon the future occurrences of that behavior. More specifically, if we follow a behavior with a reward, that is, something valued and positive, the recipient becomes more likely (i.e., motivated) to repeat that behavior in the future. To the contrary, following a behavior with a punishment, something unpleasant or painful, decreases the likelihood of that behavior going forward. When done purposely to shape someone's behavior, we call this behavior modification. It is the principle behind the boss giving bonuses to the employees at the end of the year (a reward), the cop giving a ticket to a speeding motorist (a punishment), and parents giving both timeouts (a punishment) and M&M's (a reward) to shape their child's pro-social behavior.

That's exactly what my student did to me. And that's what I did with Neil, one of my recalcitrant patients who repeatedly balked from doing his between-session psychotherapy assignments. Witness the following conversation he and I had:

DR. G: So, Neil, how are we going to get you to follow through on your between-session work? You know that you'll never get better if you don't practice what we talk about in here in your real life.

NEIL: I know, I know. I just don't have a clue what it'll take.

DR. G.: Well how about this? Suppose we use rewards and punishments?

NEIL: Meaning?

DR. G: Meaning that you reward yourself for doing your self- therapy, but punish yourself for not doing it. How about it?

NEIL: Okay.

DR. G: So, what's some pleasure you have available every day and some painful thing that's also available daily?

NEIL: That's easy. I love television. I relax every evening in front of the boob tube.

DR. G.: Good. Then let's make this rule: you reward yourself with TV after you've done your therapy work. First therapy, then TV. No work, no TV. Will you follow through on that?

NEIL: Yes!

DR. G.: Excellent. Now what about a punishment? What's something onerous you could punish yourself with if you don't do the work?

NEIL: That's easy. I hate to talk to my mother-in-law on the phone. She's so … yuck!

DR. G.: So, then, if you don't do the therapy work by 8:00 PM, you call her and chat for a minimum of at least fifteen minutes.

NEIL: That's a fate worse than death.

DR. G.: Got it, but it's an incentive, along with your reward, for doing your daily therapy. Remember: you can always watch television and never have to call dear old mom-in-law if you just choose to do the work. Clear?

NEIL: Clear.

You too can use rewards and punishments to motivate yourself to follow through on your Happiness Action Plan. Below, note both rewards you can use to reinforce your following through and punishments you can use if you don't. Then, like Neil, detail your plan of action.

Rewards for action: _____

_____

_____

Punishments for not acting: _____

_____

My plan to use rewards and punishments: _____
_____
_____

Strategy 3: Destroy Action Killing Beliefs

Negative thoughts can and will deter you from acting on your Happiness Action Plan. While any negative ones can inhibit you, five seem to crop up over and over in people who don't follow through. If you find yourself plagued by any of these, you'll want to do your best to rid yourself of them.

1. Low Frustration Tolerance (LFT)

LFT beliefs cause you to overreact to any hardship, setback, or hassle. They make you want to avoid difficult challenges and throw in the towel when you hit a roadblock. People who hold these beliefs tend to think along the following lines:

- This is *too hard*.
- It's *horrible* to have to put in this effort.
- I *can't stand* doing this.

Note how self-defeating these thoughts are. They prompt you to give up in the face of adversity and avoid the hard, sustained work of bringing about happiness, and cut corners. Try changing them to more realistic ways of thinking, as per:

- This is hard, but it's *not too hard*.
- It may be a hassle but *it certainly isn't a horror*.
- I may not always enjoy the effort, but *I certainly can stand it*.

2. Negativity

Negativity is the essence of the glass half empty thinking. With the option of looking on either the positive or negative side of things, the person locked into negativity sees only the bad but not the good, what's wrong but not what's right, what won't work rather than the possibility that it might. Thinking along these lines renders him or her discouraged, hopeless, and powerless, the kinds of moods that block any and all constructive action.

The antidote to negativity is not blind Pollyanna thinking, but realistic positivity. That is, while not denying the difficulties you face and the fact that there are no guarantees for success, you would be better off thinking things like: "Nothing ventured, nothing gained." "While I may go down in flames, I could succeed, if not this time, then the next." "I'll give it my best shot and see what happens."

3. Self-Doubt

To quote Richard Bach (Bach, 1989, p. 75), "Argue for your limitations and they are yours." Self-doubting self-talk, such as "I can't do this," "It's too much for me," or "I'm too weak to pull this off," will cripple your effort. It is true that some tasks will prove too difficult or hard for you to complete, but not the ones in this book. Furthermore, this kind of thinking will only serve to block you from even trying. That's a sure formula for failure.

As I said in my book, *Developing Unrelenting Drive, Dedication, and Determination* (Grieger, 2017, p. 104),

> Self-doubt cripples drive. It obliterates the sustained, relentless effort to produce great results. Clearly, self-doubting beliefs need to be replaced with self-confident ones ... self-confidence is not a grandiose belief in one's superstardom. Rather, it has to do with a realist appreciation of one's intelligence, ability, and experience; when one finds oneself in virgin territory, one believes in one's integrity, ability to problem solve, and grit. Self-confidence then provides the springboard for action, action, action.

4. Perfectionism

Perfectionism can drive one to success, but it can also serve to put the brakes on initiative and effort. After all, if a person demands the very best from oneself, not every once in a while, but always, then each and every effort can seem too insurmountable to even try. Here are some variations of the perfectionistic theme regarding happiness:

- I *must* be happy all the time.
- I *must* do all my strategies perfectly.
- I *must* look good and happy to everyone.

These kinds of thoughts will make you discouraged before you even make an effort. They are an exact formula for avoidance. You would be wise to replace these demands for perfection with ones that show humility, such as: "All I can do is the best I can do." "I'll give it my best shot and see what happens." "If this strategy doesn't work, I'll just keep trying until I succeed." These humble attitudes open the door to all out action without fear of failure.

5. Resentment

Resentment is one of the prime killers of all-out effort. For, when a person thinks, "I shouldn't have to work at being happy," or "I'm a good person and I deserve to be happy without all this damn effort," he or she will bitterly balk at making the effort needed to secure a daily dose of happiness. I know that's true of me when I feel bitter. I'll bet it's true of you as well.

We would be wise to eliminate all vestiges of resentment from our thinking. This requires us to give up the silly idea that we deserve to be happy without effort, that the world and the people in it shouldn't be difficult at times, and that things should always come easy. We do not have to like these harsh realities, but we would be wise to come to terms with the fact that life can be difficult, and that, alas, we are not a special case whereby we can expect that all our wishes and wants will be delivered to our front door like the Domino's pizza we order online.

So, these are the five action-killing beliefs that need to be destroyed in order for you to devote the time and energy necessary to do what's necessary to live a happy life. To rid yourself of these irrational beliefs requires you to act like a bounty hunter – that is, track them down and destroy them. Then this requires a three-step process, as shown below.

Step One: Listen For Your Killer Beliefs. As you go about your Happiness Action Plan, be alert to any Killer Beliefs that cross your mind. Be especially attentive to low frustration tolerance, negativity, self-doubt, perfectionism, and resentment self-talks. Put them into sentence form, as if you consciously thought them out.

Killer Beliefs

1. _____

   _____

   _____

2. _____
_____
_____
3. _____
_____
_____

Step Two: Destroy Their Validity. Thoughtfully think through the validity of your Killer Beliefs until you can clearly see its absurdity. Take each in turn and challenge them with the following three questions:

Killer Belief: _____
_____
_____

Is this belief true or valid? How so? _____
_____
_____

How do I react when I hold this belief – Emotionally? Behaviorally? Does this reaction help me or would I be better off without this belief? How so?

_____
_____
_____

Step Three: New Empowering Belief. Once you have shown yourself how self-defeating your Killer Belief is, you then come up with a new one that will aid and abet your ability to act on your Happiness Action Plan.

What's a better, more empowering belief that would help me produce the happiness results I want? _____
_____
_____

Strategy 4: Use Empowering Affirmations

One of my close friends is a hypnotherapist. He first induces a relaxed, receptive state (a hypnotic trance, he calls it), and then he provides empowering affirmations to his patient to help them relieve their suffering. He explains that, by doing this, he can break through stubborn defenses, overpowering emotions, and negative thinking in order to implant rational thoughts into the patient's consciousness.

You may not be a hypnotherapist, but you can certainly build positive, empowering affirmations into the fabric of your everyday thinking. I do this every morning before I start my day. Some of mine include: "Today is an opportunity to make a positive impact on people's lives." "I have so much to be grateful for that I am one lucky guy." "Act boldly today because the worst thing that will happen is I'll fail, and that's no big deal."

With regard to bringing pleasure, satisfaction, and happiness into your life through the use of your Action Plan, here are a few examples. Please feel free to crib them exactly as I've stated them, alter them to fit your situation, or even make up ones of your own.

- "I'm worth it. I owe it to myself to bring as much pleasure and satisfaction as I reasonably can to my day."
- "This is the only life I know for certain I am ever going to have. Don't waste even one day. Go for it."
- "Be bold and go for it. The worst thing that will happen is that I'll fail. So what. Nothing ventured, nothing gained. Besides, I can always learn from my mistakes and do better tomorrow."

Now here's your opportunity. With some thought, below write up to three affirmations you can use to stimulate you to act on your Happiness Action Plan:

1. _____
   _____
   _____
   _____

2. _____
   _____
   _____
   _____

3. _____
   _____
   _____
   _____

Strategy 5: Build a Support Team

When I first meet new patients, I try my best to give them hope by convincing them of two things: one, they can and will get better, so long, that is, as they work hard, both in and between our therapy sessions; and two, they are not alone, as I will be working hard alongside them every step of the way.

The truth is that we live in in an interdependent world, one in which we can accomplish so much more with the help and support of others, as opposed to when we work alone or, worse, in conflict. This is true in the worlds of sports, business, and families, to name but just a few arenas.

In this vein, you would be wise to form your very own support team in your quest for happiness. Who in your family might you enroll – your significant other? Your brother or sister? Who among your close friends might support you? What about an organized group of people in the community? These trusted others can help you clarify fuzzy concerns, give you precious support, hold you accountable for follow through, give you valuable feedback, and pat you on the back for a job well done.

Now is an opportunity for you to craft your own support team. Note below who you will enroll and exactly what you'll ask them to do to support you in your quest for happiness. All you have to do is invite them aboard.

My support person(s): _____

_____

_____

_____

What will I ask this person(s) to do: _____

_____

_____

_____

Your Psychological Sustaining Action Plan

Never forget that your happiness is 100% your responsibility. With that in mind, consider which of the psychological strategies discussed in this chapter might help you sustain your efforts to bring happiness into your life. For each, write exactly what you will do and when and where you will do it.

	Strategy	What	Where/When
1.	_____	_____	_____
	_____	_____	_____
2.	_____	_____	_____
	_____	_____	_____

Going Forward

It is my hope that the work you've done in this chapter will help you sustain the effort needed to bring happiness to most all of your days. Just remember that you are worth the effort. Despite your success with these, I urge you to forge ahead to Chapter 11: "Sustaining Happiness Action: The Philosophical Way." It is the granddaddy of all sustained effort. See you when you get there.

Notes

_____

_____

_____

_____

_____

_____

_____

_____

_____

_____

_____

_____

_____

_____

_____

_____

_____

_____

_____

_____

_____

_____

_____

_____

_____

_____

_____

_____

_____

_____

_____

_____

_____

11

SUSTAINING HAPPINESS ACTION

The Philosophical Way

George Bernard Shaw got it exactly right. People who succeed in producing the results they want power forward. They act, act, and then act some more until they meet their goal, regardless of any and all difficult circumstances they may encounter. Those who don't often fold when they bump up against adversity.

I demonstrate this notion in my personal empowerment workshops through a three-part exercise. Pretend that you're in the room working right alongside all the other participants.

To begin, I instruct them to recall three recent situations in which they made a commitment to produce some result but did not follow through to success. I explain that these broken promises can be ones made either to another or to themselves, given thoughtfully or impulsively, or be consequential or trivial. Then, for each broken promise, I tell them to note the reasons they gave to excuse, explain away, or rationalize why they did not produce the result.

Now you do it. Note below three recent commitments you did not fulfill and then write the reason you used to explain why you didn't follow through.

	Broken Promise	**Reason**
1.	_____	_____
	_____	_____
2.	_____	_____
	_____	_____
3.	_____	_____
	_____	_____

Most of my workshop participants have little trouble identifying three such examples as, I'm sure, was true for you as well. After all, they, and you, are only human. But Step Two is when the fun begins. This is when I assemble them into threesomes and challenge them as a group to figure out how they each could have kept all three of their broken promises despite the adverse circumstances they let block them.

This is what I want you to do right now. Figure out exactly how you could have kept all three of your broken promises despite the difficulties, hassles, or inconveniences you faced. Be rigorous. Be hard-nosed. Don't let yourself off the hook. Go for it.

1. _____   _____

    _____   _____

2. _____   _____

    _____   _____

3. _____   _____

    _____   _____

I've yet to see it fail. With a little prompting, most everyone finds that they could have kept all three of their commitments if only they had bothered to do so. Wasn't that true for you as well? It might have been difficult for you to keep your commitment. It may have been frustrating. It may have prevented you from enjoying some other pleasurable activity. But you proved that you could have done it, if you had only been willing. Right?

Assuming that I'm correct, I've now backed them, and you, into a corner. Like you, they each made three promises to produce some intended result but did not follow through. Instead, they produced reasons – explanations, rationalizations, excuses. But both they and you proved that, indeed, the promises could have been honored if only you had been willing to do what was necessary to do so.

I've now led you all to the third part of the exercise – the moment of truth. The questions I now ask are: Why didn't you keep your word? What kept you from honoring your promises? What stopped you from producing your committed results?

No matter the group, the participants almost always voice the same three answers: (1) to keep the commitment would have caused them some hardship or hassle; (2) their priorities changed over time such that something else became more important; (3) they no longer felt motivated. Do any of these fit your examples?

What these answers illustrate, I then explain, is that they (and maybe you also) found themselves in the grip of what I call the principle of Conditional Personal Responsibility. That is, when they initially made their commitments, they fully intended on honoring them. But, in the back of their mind lurked an escape hatch. That is, they held that, if the circumstances in and around them at the moment of truth made it easy and convenient for them to keep their word, they would indeed act to produce the results. But, if not, they could justifiably throw in the towel and then give reasons why they didn't do the job rather than produce the promised outcome. They based their behavior on the circumstances, not their word. What they all needed, and maybe this is true for you as well, is a healthy dose of the philosophy of Unconditional Personal Responsibility (UPR).

Unconditional Personal Responsibility is the philosophical granddaddy of all committed action. By mastering this paradigm, you will be absolutely dedicated to sustaining the effort necessary to produce promised results, happiness in this case, despite the intrusion of such circumstances as the ups and downs of your enthusiasm, unexpected hassles or hardships, or even any your own personal shortcomings.

Does this sound pie-in-the-sky? It's not. Many, many people have produced wondrous results simply by adopting this philosophical paradigm. So can you. Let me now flesh out for you, as I do for them, exactly what is Unconditional Personal Responsibility.

Defining Unconditional Personal Responsibility

At the outset, it's important to emphasize that UPR does not refer to a tangible chore or duty, such as keeping your lawn mowed, driving within the speed limit, or paying your taxes. Rather, it is a profound philosophical principle that you will either adopt and live by or not. Read carefully the following definition created by the EST Foundation (Bartley, 1978), then I'll do my best to help you make sense of it.

Responsibility starts with the **willingness** to experience your **self** as **cause**. It starts with the willingness to have the experience of your **self** as **cause** in the matter.

Responsibility starts with the **willingness** to deal with a situation from and with the point of view, whether at the moment realized or not, that you are the **cause**, or source, of what you are, what you do, and what you have.

Ultimately, responsibility is a principle – a principle of **self** as source – for what you choose to do.

Notice that I highlight in bold three concepts in this definition – willingness, self, and cause. Let's take a look at each.

Willingness. Unconditional Personal Responsibility starts with a person being willing to do what is necessary to keep one's commitments and produce promised results, within of course, the confines of ethics, morals, and the law As opposed to trying, which focuses on effort, not results, willingness emphasizes no-holds-barred doing until the intended results are produced. No matter what are the difficult or onerous circumstances, one willfully persists past, through, and over obstacles until intended results are created.

When you think of willingness, you might think of basketball great, Michael Jordan, or Thomas Edison, the inventor of the light bulb, or comedian, Steve Martin. Each of these superstars willingly persisted, persisted, and then persisted some more in the pursuit of their intended results until they finally created them. They lived, probably without even realizing it, by the paradigm of Unconditional Personal Responsibility.

Self. You may remember that the first sentence of the definition of Unconditional Personal Responsibility reads, "Responsibility starts with the willingness to experience your *self* as cause." In this definition, self refers to you. It communicates that you, and no one else, are the source of whatever you do and don't do – not other people, your current mood, your degree of motivation, your current physical state, or the circumstances that exist about you. I am sitting at my desk writing this book because I chose to; if I were not writing, I would have chosen that. You are reading this book because you chose to; if you are not, then you chose that as well.

You see, barring some extraordinary circumstances, such as suffering a severe brain injury, being incapacitated by a debilitating heart attack, or held in the grip of some dissociative disorder, you always have a choice. This holds true not only with regard to relatively inconsequential matters, such as deciding whether to order a Big Mac or Chicken McNuggets, but also with regard to major issues, such as whether or not to dive into an icy water to rescue a drowning toddler. This basic truth – that I am the chooser of virtually every choice that I choose – is one of the most empowering insights a person can uncover. For, when one takes responsibility for one's choices, one claims the power to choose to do what is necessary to produce desired results. Just ask Michael Jordan, Thomas Edison, and Steve Martin if this wasn't so for them.

These two UPR ingredients – willingness and self – take us to the last component of Unconditional Personal Responsibility: Cause. It is one of the most empowering concepts you will ever encounter.

Cause. In the world of personal responsibility, there is a critical distinction between the paradigm of *Cause*, more completely stated as *Being at Cause*, the essence of Unconditional Personal Responsibility, and *Effect*, or *Being at Effect*, the paradigm of Conditional Personal Responsibility. To truly grasp Being at Cause, let's first flesh out Being at Effect. Being at Effect can be captured by the following principal (Grieger, 2017, p. 18):

> How I act, the choices I make, and the results I produce, ultimately depend on the circumstances operating at the time. So, when I give my word to do something or commit to producing some result, I do mean it. I'm not lying. But, I hold, in the back of my mind, that, if some circumstance arises that makes it difficult or unpleasant to keep my promise, that circumstance justifies not keeping it.

By way of example, consider your Happiness Action Plan. Let's say that you committed to do the daily activities you outlined. You are enthusiastic, even fired up to follow through today. But, say, tomorrow, you wake up tired, perhaps with a backache, maybe in a bad mood. Being at Effect, you conclude that these inner circumstances make it acceptable to lay low and do nothing constructive for the day. This hardly makes you a lazy person, but it does not forward your goal of experiencing happiness one bit.

So, Being at Effect is a belief, a principal, in which one holds one's promises or commitments as always breakable or bendable, depending on the outer or inner circumstances that exist at the point of taking action. If you find the circumstances favorable, you act; if not, you choose to not act. What then do you do? You then offer excuses ("I'm too tired."), rationalizations ("My back is killing me."), or reasons ("Life just sucks."). One lost day may be inconsequential to your overall happiness, but imagine the massive cost to your happiness over a lifetime of acting according to this way of thinking.

As illustrated in Table 11.1, Being at Cause is central to Unconditional Personal Responsibility. It is about holding your word – your promises and commitments – as the highest principle in your ethical system. It is about making choices outside circumstances. It means that your promises and commitments are the driving force of your choices, not how you feel or what exists out there with regard to people, places, or things. It means being willing to do what it

Table 11.1 BAC/BAE Dichotomy

Being at Cause vs. Being at Effect	
(Unconditional Personal Responsibility)	*(Conditional Personal Responsibility)*
• Live by your word/commitment • Live by your character - your principles • No excuses valid or acceptable; only results • Results on purpose • Most likely happy	• Live by circumstances • Live by your psychology - feelings, desires, and habits • Excuses instead of results are acceptable • Results by luck, hope, or prayer • May be happy

takes to produce promised results, no matter what the circumstances. It means living by the following psychobabble-free definition of responsibility.

> "Responsibility is **a belief** in which one holds oneself **100% responsible** for honoring one's promises and commitments and producing intended results no matter how hard it may be.
>
> Responsibility is being **100% willing** to rise above difficult circumstances to achieve the results one promises. It is a belief in which one continually asks: 'What else can I do to overcome these obstacles and problems and keep my promised and committed results?'
>
> Ultimately, responsibility is a **belief** one holds that says, 'My word is my bond, and I will keep my word even when it is tough to do so.'"

To sum, Unconditional Personal Responsibility is guided by the following five key perspectives.

1. *You are driven by your word* – your promises and commitments – not by the inner circumstances of your psychology – your desire of the moment, your motivational state, your physical comfort – or the outer circumstances surrounding you – the telephone, other people, the traffic.
2. Neither the size of your commitment, not how important it may be, nor to whom it was made (including yourself) makes a difference. *What matters is the fact that you made a commitment.* Once made, no circumstance justifies not keeping it.
3. Once a promise is given or a commitment is made, *your focus is on no-holds-barred doing.* Your attitude is: (1) I will *do* what I need to do to keep my promise; (2) I will willingly *persist* until I fulfill all the conditions of my promise.

Remember what Albert Einstein once famously said, "Genius is 10% inspiration and 90% perspiration."

4. *Obstacles are never game-breakers.* They are merely circumstances to overcome to produce the promised results. The questions a person who endorses UPR repeatedly asks are: What else can I do? How can I overcome this obstacle and produce my commitment results? Who or what do I need to enlist if I can't do it on my own?

5. *Carefully choose what promises you make.* But, once you make them, hold them sacred and fulfill them.

Happiness on Purpose

Now is your opportunity to use the philosophy of Unconditional Personal Responsibility to help you relentlessly pursue your Happiness Action Plan. If you decide to do so, please do it with total integrity for you can have a profound impact on your happiness quotient.

Before beginning, however I want to assert two things. One, in the domain of personal responsibility, there are two, and only two, choices: (1) Unconditional Personal Responsibility – Being at Cause; (2) Conditional Personal Responsibility – Being at Effect. These are the only two choices you have. In any situation, you can only Be at Cause or Be at Effect. That's it.

Second, simply by the fact of being alive and possessing an intact human brain, you cannot not make the choices between Conditional and Unconditional Personal Responsibility. In other words, in each moment of your life, whether you realize it or not, you will endorse and live out one or the other of these principles, thereby getting the results, or not, of the paradigm you choose. You simply cannot not play the personal responsibility game.

What follows, then, are five Unconditional Personal Responsibility strategies you can adopt to help you follow through on your Happiness Action Plan. Pick ones that you think may be of use to you.

Commit to Your Commitments

Strategy One is straightforward and simple. It calls for you to consciously and purposely make a decision as to which of these two paradigms you will adopt in order to bring about your happiness. Below are the two choices you have – Conditional Personal Responsibility and Unconditional Personal Responsibility. Choose wisely as your choice will have profound repercussions with regard to your future happiness.

I, _____, take full responsibility for and fully commit to acting on my Happiness Action Plan, except when the circumstances I face make it difficult for me to do so.

Signed _____

Date _____

I, _____, take full responsibility for and fully commit to acting on my happiness action plan. I will do so despite any and all adverse circumstances.

Signed _____

Date _____

Rid Adverse Circumstances

It is obvious that difficult circumstances will arise that make it difficult for you to follow through on your Happiness Action Plan. But you need not be their victim. You can proactively act to rid them from your life. Identify below both inner and outer circumstances that you tend to let deter you from following through on your HAP. For each, write an UPR message that can prompt you to act rather than rationalize why it's too hard to do.

Inner Circumstances	UPR Self-Talk

- **Negative Feelings States:**

_____ _____

_____ _____

- **Diminished Motivation:**

_____ _____

_____ _____

- **Adverse Physical States:**

_____ _____

_____ _____

Outer Circumstances	UPR Self-Talk
• **People:**	
_____	_____
_____	_____
• **Places:**	
_____	_____
_____	_____
• **Situations:**	
_____	_____
_____	_____

Build Your UPR Muscle

Living by your word can be difficult at first. After all, most all of us conduct our lives by the principle of Conditional Personal Responsibility without even being aware of it.

Accordingly, you can approach UPR muscle building in two ways. The first I call transformational. This means that you go all out – you determine to keep all your commitments, 100%, no-holds-barred, from this moment going forward.

The alternative approach I call developmental. This means that you gradually build your UPR muscle one step at a time. You start by first working on one commitment; as you master the keeping of this one, then you add another, then another, and then another until you find yourself keeping all your commitments as a matter of course. As you climb the ladder, you keep an eye on your CPR/BAE self-talk and instantly refute it.

Ladder of Success	CPR Self Talk	UPR Rebuttal
1. _____	_____	_____
_____	_____	_____
2. _____	_____	_____
_____	_____	_____

3. _____ _____ _____

    _____ _____ _____

4. _____ _____ _____

    _____ _____ _____

5. _____ _____ _____

    _____ _____ _____

Put Teeth in Your Promises

The fact of the matter is that we often make weak promises. How often do we say, "I'll see," "I'll do my best," and the ever popular, "I'll try." Stripped of the verbiage, they amount to wishes, hopes, even maybe's, but not full-blown commitments.

Going forward, make it a point to make promises that have teeth, ones that clearly communicate that you fully and unconditionally intend on keeping your word. Promises with teeth sound like this: "I promise (you) that I will do X by time Y." Notice that this formula contains these elements.

- "I" – You are willing to take a stand and be committed to producing promised results.
- "Promise" – By using the word, "promise," you take a stand. You have put your integrity on the line. You have stated, in no uncertain terms, a no-holds-barred commitment. Similar words to "promise" would be: Pledge, swear, assure, guarantee, commit, and the like.
- "I will" – "I will" underscores your willingness to do what is necessary to produce the promised results.
- "X by time Y" – There are conditions of satisfaction – They tell you exactly what you promise to do and precisely when you will deliver. This leaves no wiggle room, telling the receiver of the promise exactly what to expect.

Practice making powerful promises. You can plan to do so below. These will first alert you to the fact that you are making a promise, rather than doing so as a casual throw-away, and leave no doubt in your mind exactly what you are committing to produce.

Result To Be Produced	Powerful Promise
1. _____	_____
_____	_____
2. _____	_____
_____	_____
3. _____	_____
_____	_____
4. _____	_____
_____	_____
5. _____	_____
_____	_____

Do a Daily Check-In

I start off each morning by reviewing my upcoming day. Not only do I ground myself in my Passionate Purpose (see Chapter 5), but I also make note of that day's commitments. This provides me an opportunity to re-commit to unconditionally produce my intended results. These few moments each morning serve me quite well with regard to my productivity across the fabric of my life.

Doing a daily check-in can likewise serve you well. Like me, you can do it first thing in the morning, anytime during the day, or even in the evening as you plan your next day. Below is an opportunity to commit to a strategy to plan your daily commitments.

My UPR Check-In Plan _____

_____

_____

_____

Going Forward

Unconditional Personal Responsibility is a character trait that can serve you well in all facets of your life – with your significant other and your family, in your job or career, with regard to your physical and mental well-being, with your friend, and in your spirituality. It can also be of benefit with regard to your happiness.

Remember the definition I offered way back in the "Introduction" to this book: "Happiness is *acting* in accordance with your passionate purpose, grounded in rational thought about yourself, other people, and life in general, and guided by your sacred principles." Notice how key the word "acting" is. Unless you act to bring happiness to your life – both physically and mentally – you will only find happiness by the luck of the draw.

Notes

EPILOGUE

While happiness is within most all of our reach, the thrust of *The Serious Business of Being Happy* is that it is up to us to bring it about.

Indeed, as you will remember from the "Introduction," I emphasized that true happiness, as opposed to transitory states of fun and pleasure, comes from purposely and relentlessly "Acting in accordance with your passionate purpose, grounded in rational thought about yourself, other people, and life in general, and guided by your sacred principals" (p. 3). With that perspective, it requires you to live by these salient mindsets:

(1) **This is it:** Take advantage of each and every day because, as far as we know, this is the one and only life we are certain we will ever have;

(2) **If it's going to be, it's up to me:** Your happiness depends on you, no one else. So, step up to the plate and take responsibility to bring it about – enthusiastically, purposely, relentlessly.

(3) **Decide to be happy:** All results start with a conscious decision to produce them. In the same vein that you made all the other important decisions in your life, also decide to do so with regard to your happiness.

(4) **Attitude is everything:** Your thinking is just as important to creating life happiness as it is to acting properly. Thus, work hard on your mindsets as well as on all the other strategies you found useful in this book.

(5) **Work, work, work:** Since very few valued results fall into our laps without plain old hard work, it's important to wrap your mind around the fact that you will need to invest effort over the long haul to bring and keep the happiness you want in your life.

Once adopted, these five mindsets provide a springboard for the sustained use of the personalized Happiness Action Plan you crafted from the proven practices I shared in Part II of this book, strategies to:

- Live your passionate purpose (Chapter 4);
- Be happy with yourself (Chapter 5);
- Be happy with others (Chapter 6);
- Be happy with your life (Chapter 7); and
- Live your ethical principles (Chapter 8).

With your Happiness Action Plan crafted and in place, all you have to do is act on it and, all things being equal, you will find your satisfaction, fulfillment, and happiness quotient rise to the level when you will be able to say, "You know, I'm happy with my happiness."

Can you do that?

I know you can.

Will you?

That I don't know. It's up to you. Go for it full bore.

A Final Word

I want to take the opportunity to let you know how honored I am to have served you through this book. It has been a pleasure to have put what you've read on paper and to have done my best to help you make your life perfect, as you want it. Thank you, thank you, thank you for the privilege.

My commitment to you does not end, however, with the last page of this book. I sincerely invite you to contact me at any time if you want to further pick my brain. To get in touch, please email me at grieger@cstone.net.

REFERENCES

Aristotle. (1955). *The ethics of Aristotle: The Nicomachean ethics* (rev. ed.) (J. K. Thomson, trans). New York, NY: Viking Press, p. 104.

Camus, A. (1942). *The stranger.* Paris, France: Librairie Gallimard.

Collins, J. (2001). *Good to great.* New York, NY: Harper Collins Publishers Inc.

Colvin, G. (2008). *Talent is overrated.* New York, NY: The Penguin Group.

Covey, S. (1989). *The 7 habits of highly effective people.* New York, NY: Simon & Schuster.

Csikszentmihalyi, M. (1991). *Finding flow.* New York: Basic Books.

Ellis, A. (1972). "Psychology and the value of a human being." In *Value and validation: Axiological studies in honor of Robert S. Hartman,* J. W. Davis (Ed.) Knoxville, TN: University of Tennessee Press.

Ellis, A. & Becker, I. (1982). *A guide to personal happiness.* N. Hollywood, CA: Wilshire Book Company.

Gladwell, M. (2008). *Outliers: The story of success.* New York, NY: Little, Brown and Company.

Grieger, R. (2017). *Developing unrelenting drive, dedication, and determination.* NY: Routledge.

Heidegger, M. (2018). *Being and time.* NY: Harper Perennials.

Levitin, D. J. (2006). *This is your brain on music: The science of human obsession.* New York: Plume/Penguin.

Rogers, C. (1951). *Client-centered therapy: Its current practice, implications and theory.* Cambridge, MA: The Riverside Press.

Sarte, J.-P. (1943). *Being and nothingness.* Éditions Gallimard, Philosophical Library.

Seligman, M. E. P. (2002). *Authentic happiness: Using the new positive psychology to realize your potential for lasting fulfillment.* New York, NY: Free Press.

Skinner, B. F. (1974). *About behaviorism.* New York, NY: Harper Collins.

INDEX

Figures are marked with *italics*, while tables are marked with **bold**.